IRISH MANAGEMENT
LIBRARY
★ INSTITUTE ★

H0654717

Creating
a Balance

aging
tress

IMI *information service*
Sandyford, Dublin 16
Telephone 2078513 Fax
email library@imi.ie
Internet http://www.im

Creating a Balance

Managing Stress

Stephen Palmer
Cary Cooper
and Kate Thomas

THE BRITISH LIBRARY

First published 2003 by
The British Library
96 Euston Road
London NW1 2DB

Copyright © The British Library Board 2003

The authors assert their moral right in the work

British Library Cataloguing in Publication Data
A Catalogue record for this book is available from The British Library

ISBN 0–7123–0892–X

Designed by Andrew Shoolbred
Typeset by Hope Services (Abingdon) Ltd
Printed in England by St Edmundsbury Press,
Bury St Edmunds

Dedications

To Prof. Arnold Lazarus who developed the multimodal approach.

To the people of Porthleven, Cornwall. You make it a great place. And, once again, to Maggie. (SP)

To my lifelong friend and mentor Prof. Sir Roland Smith. To a work colleague, Ian Haworth, for his support and encouragement over the last five years. (CC)

To my parents for the ongoing help they have given me throughout my life. And especially to Kevin, for the constant support, patience and encouragement he has shown me whilst writing this book. (KT)

Contents

Introduction: become your own stress management coach

Stress management has become a popular phrase and past-time. Often courses or self-help books only focus on one or two approaches for dealing with stress such as meditation or relaxation. Although these methods can be very beneficial, people do not always deal with their stress levels in the most appropriate or effective way.

This book has been written to provide you with the information needed to enable you to become your own stress management coach and therefore manage your life better. It gives an in-depth insight into the causes of stress and includes numerous techniques and strategies on how to deal with them throughout all stages of life; from childhood to retirement, from personal through to work relationships. The underlying premise of this book is that you may often contribute to your own stress levels. However, there is some good news. The advantage of this position is that you, as the reader, are able to reduce and manage your own stress levels.

The first two chapters of the book focus on definitions of stress, its physiology, and a model that illustrates seven aspects of stress. The following chapters take each of these seven responses in turn and contain tips and methods to deal with them. Throughout the book there are a number of case studies, exercises and questionnaires. These will allow you to relate the theories and ideas to your own personal life. Many of the techniques and strategies discussed in these chapters are not unique to one stress response. Instead they overlap and can often be used to manage a variety of responses. Chapter 10 looks at a self-profile enabling you to identify how you respond to stress and draw up your own action plan to reduce your stress levels. It takes into account your scores from the various questionnaires throughout the book.

Chapters 11 to 14 concentrate on how to deal with stress in key stages of our lives, from stress in children through to retirement. There is also a chapter on managing stress at work.

However, at this stage it is important to point out a major caveat. If at anytime when using one of the strategies or techniques described in this book you experience high levels of anxiety or you find them unhelpful, please stop using them. Similarly, if you have physical or psychological symptoms that you have not had diagnosed, consult a medical professional. Seek help – you do not have to suffer alone. If you are experiencing high levels of stress, we would recommend you talk to an experienced psychologist or therapist. There are a list of useful contacts and organisations in the appendix. Throughout the book, we have provided references in case you wish to follow-up where we have obtained our information. In addition to the numerous case studies which illustrate a wide range of problems we have provided examples of how the different techniques are applied to a specific problem, presentation stress. This highlights how we can find successful solutions using a variety of strategies.

This book contains all the information you need to manage your stress and become your own stress management coach – enabling you to live a more relaxed and enjoyable life if you so wish!

The approach advocated by this book is based on the work of many practitioners and researchers, in particular, Professor Arnold Lazarus (1989; 1997), Dr Aaron Beck (1993), Dr Albert Ellis (Ellis, 1997; 2001; Ellis et al., 1997), Professor Richard Lazarus (1999), Michael Neenan (Neenan and Dryden, 2002), as well as two of its authors, Professor Cary Cooper and Professor Stephen Palmer.

What is stress?

We all suffer from stress at some point in our lives. It is estimated to cost UK employers around £370 million and society as a whole about £3.75 billion (1995/96 prices, HSE, 2001). However, the Confederation of British Industry estimates the cost of stress to be about £5.2 billion. Approximately, 360 million working days are lost each year in the UK as a result of stress. Many courses run in public and private organisations help people to reduce stress. People talk about stress in every day conversation with work colleagues, family and friends. In fact, often in the past few years you cannot pick up a newspaper or a magazine without seeing it mentioned.

What is this phenomenon: stress? The word in itself is commonly known and used. Yet frequently the complexities of stress are not fully understood. Not only can stress result in ineffective and inefficient working practices, it can also seriously affect people's health and impact on their relationships with other people both at work and home, throughout their lives.

And yet we live in a society in which stress is a fact of life. In a recent study carried out for the International Stress Management Association (ISMA UK, 2000) about one-third of the interviewees said they found it stressful balancing their work and home lives. This comes as no surprise because in this day and age we are expected to work longer hours; there is not the same level of job security that there once was, and there are the pressures incurred by the modern technologies that require things to be done faster and more efficiently.

In our personal lives we are all likely to experience one of the life events that can lead to stress such as the death of someone close, the break-up of a relationship, or even surprisingly a holiday.

And our work and home life interact. The reality is that a person experiencing stress at home is likely to have less concentration at work, thus affecting their performance. Similarly, an employee facing stressful challenges in the workplace may be unable to switch off at home, potentially impacting on their personal relationships. It is therefore not surprising that the word 'stress' is referred to so frequently.

So how do we deal with these circumstances and reach a healthy balance between our personal and work lives?

This book will endeavour to answer this question by looking at all aspects of life from childhood to studying; from personal relationships to retirement; and through to work. It will not only explain how we deal with stress, it will also explain why we respond in certain ways when under stress. And finally it offers some practical advice and tips on how to manage your stress better, and therefore become your own stress coach providing invaluable help as you go through your life.

Definitions of stress

The word 'stress' has a number of derivations. One is from the Middle English word *stresse*, meaning hardship and distress. Another is from the Latin word *stringere*, meaning to tighten or press. Both imply a feeling of pressure and difficulty, akin to what we often describe as modern day stress.

More recently there have been a number of definitions developed by psychologists. One simple example is by R.S. Lazarus and S. Folkman (1984) who describe stress as an imbalance between demands and resources. However, this definition does not attribute any responsibility to the way in which you perceive the demands and resources. In life, demands are placed on you all the time and different people will react to them in different ways. Therefore the way in which you perceive these pressures will play a part in the way in which you deal with or cope with them.

Perhaps a more accurate definition is: 'Stress occurs when the perceived pressure exceeds your perceived ability to cope'. So it is not simply the external pressure, such as giving a presentation or going on holiday abroad, which triggers stress, but whether you believe you can cope with the situation.

For an experienced presenter the level of stress is likely to be far less than the person who has never given a presentation before. Similarly, for a person who flies regularly, going on holiday will be less daunting than for someone who only has the occasional trip abroad. In addition to these factors, if you do not perceive the situation to be important or threatening, you are unlikely to feel particularly stressed if you do not deal with it successfully. Thus using a new item of cutlery incorrectly is unlikely to trigger stress!

Stress experienced in the workplace can be further defined as 'the harmful physical and emotional responses that occur when the requirements of the job do not match the capabilities, resources, or needs of the worker' (Stress at work – NIOSH, 1999). The UK's Health and Safety Executive (2001) has a similar definition of work-related stress: 'The adverse reaction people have to excessive pressures or other types of demand placed on them'.

Our view of stress is that it is not simply caused by an interaction between the external world and yourself, but by your own perceptions towards situations you find yourself in throughout life. Stress is different to everyday pressures and challenges you face in your personal life or at work. The right amount of personal pressure can encourage you to perform at your best. For example to:

- organise everything required for your house move
- book that long overdue family holiday or
- deal with your children leaving home to go to university.

And work challenges can provide both the stimulus to:

- learn new skills and
- improve your job performance.

When you meet these pressures or challenges it is likely you will feel personal satisfaction. It is when you are not able to cope with these pressures and challenges that you will begin to experience stress.

The idea that our perception impacts upon our stress levels is not new. The Stoic philosopher, Epictetus claimed almost two thousand years ago: 'People are disturbed not by things but by the views which they take of them.' A second century stoic, Marcus Aurelius stated in his now famous, *Meditations* (1995): 'Put from you the belief that "I have been wronged", and with it will go the feeling. Reject your sense of injury, and the injury itself disappears'. Similarly, William Shakespeare wrote: 'Why, then 'tis none to you; for there is nothing either good or bad, but thinking makes it so...' (Hamlet, II.ii 247–8). Our approach to stress and its management therefore takes a neo-stoic view.

Figure 1 highlights the relationship between pressure and being able to cope. It is useful to use the diagram to check regularly where you are. When you are working at your optimum level you will be less likely to suffer from stress. In fact, it really feels good to work at your optimum. You look forward to the day ahead.

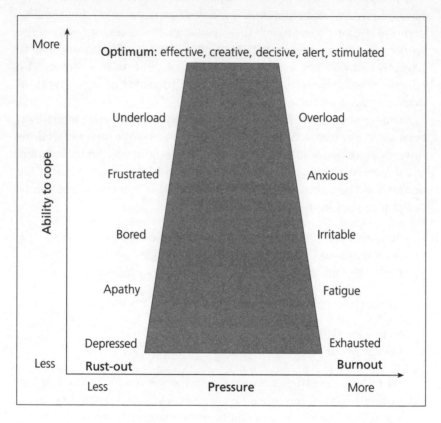

Figure 1: The relationship of pressure to the ability to cope
(adapted from Palmer & Strickland, 1996)

Physiology of stress

This section explains the physiology of the stress response. If the physiological aspects of stress are not of interest please feel free to skip this part and go onto the model of stress explained in Chapter 2.

When you find yourself in a situation you perceive as threatening, your nervous system responds to deal with this problem. The cerebral cortex in your brain signals to the hypothalamus to prepare for 'flight or fight'. This is the same response that helped your ancestors to survive when faced, say, with a pack of wolves.

The hypothalamus then passes a signal to every part of your body via three interrelated, yet separate systems, the nervous, endocrine and immune systems. This serves to prepare you further for the physical action that may be required in order to survive the stressful situation. The anterior hypothalamus produces arousal of the autonomic nervous system (ANS). The ANS is an automatic system that controls the heart, lungs, stomach, blood vessels and glands. The ANS consists of two different systems: the sympathetic nervous system and the parasympathetic nervous system (Toates,1995). Essentially, the parasympathetic nervous system conserves energy levels and aids relaxation. Whereas the sympathetic nervous system prepares the body for action. In a stressful situation, it quickly causes your body to react in the following ways (Gregson and Looker, 1996):

- Your heart starts to beat faster and with greater force (providing you with more blood containing oxygen and nutrients).
- Your lungs begin to breathe more quickly (ensuring an increase of oxygen into the blood and carbon dioxide out).
- The adrenals release the stress hormones adrenaline and noradrenaline which increase the frequency and strength of heart contractions.
- The blood vessels leading to your heart and other major muscles dilate providing them with the necessary increase in fuels needed in a threatening situation. This is caused by adrenaline.
- Noradrenaline causes the constriction of specific blood vessels resulting in a decrease of blood flow to the digestive system and the peripheral circulation, which are not as important in the event of an emergency.
- The adrenals release the steroid, cortisol which reduces inflammation, allowing damaged joints to continue being used. Cortisol helps to make glucose available, but by slowing its metabolism or use, glucose is kept in reserve. Cortisol also simulates the breakdown of fats (Toates, 1995). However, over a long period of time raised levels of cortisol have a detrimental effect on the immune system as is the case with long-term stress.

These preparatory activities happen automatically, and enhance your ability to deal with the threatening situation. In other words, these physiological responses promote the 'survival of the fittest' and in the case of the pack of wolves increase the chance of either fighting them off or escaping from them. Once the perceived threat is over, the body returns to its original state of equilibrium.

Obviously, these days very few of us are confronted with a pack of wolves! Yet, these are the same physiological responses that occur every time you find yourself in a situation you perceive as stressful. From an evolutionary perspective, this 'flight or fight' response evolved to deal with these one-off events such as aggression from predators, but generally, either fighting or running away are not the best ways to deal with modern-day challenges such as the computer crashing. Therefore, if a person continues to perceive a situation as stressful, their body will continue to react as if they are under threat.

If this state of threat is sustained over a long period of time the person will be putting their body through enormous amounts of strain and they will be in danger of developing long-term stress-related problems as their immune system may be repressed (Leonard and Miller, 1995). It is important to remember that in extreme and prolonged circumstances stress can lead to a number of medical conditions from high blood pressure, cancer, heart attacks and strokes, to psychological disorders such as breakdowns or depression. There are also a number of behavioural problems such as alcoholism and increased aggression.

2

A model of stress

Traditionally the responses of stress are broken down into three categories:

- psychological
- physiological
- behavioural.

However, our model of stress breaks these three categories down into seven discrete responses, sometimes known as modalities. Figure 2 explains the relationship between the external stress-inducing factor and the seven possible reactions to it. The responses are:

- **Behavioural** (how you act)
- **Affect/Emotional** (how you feel)
- **Sensory** (physical feeling)
- **Imagery** (images and pictures)
- **Cognitive** (beliefs, thoughts, perceptions and attitudes)
- **Interpersonal** (how you relate to others)
- **Drug-related/Biological** (medical and biological responses)

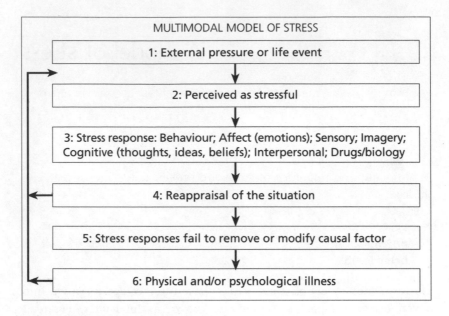

Figure 2: Multomodal model of stress
(adapted from Palmer and Strickland, 1996; Palmer, 1997)

This model follows the Multimodal Approach developed by Professor Arnold Lazarus (1989; 1997) and later applied to the field of stress management by Professor Stephen Palmer (1996; 1997a; Palmer and Dryden, 1991; 1995). The approach rests on the assumption that unless all seven responses or modalities are considered, a successful outcome may not occur as significant issues may be overlooked by the person suffering from stress. The first letters of the seven responses form the acronym: BASIC I.D. The first part is easy to remember, BASIC, and the second part I.D. reminds people of identity. For the purposes of this book we have developed the BASIC I.D. principles and related them to the management of stress using techniques to deal with problems arising in the seven responses.

Stage 1 is the external pressure or life event. This can include a number of different factors and will vary for every individual. For example, attending a job interview may be stressful for one person, but not for another. Alternatively, dealing with children leaving home may be stressful for someone else, whereas another parent may look forward to being able to have more space around the house once the children have left home. In other words, this pressure can be any factor that an individual perceives as stressful.

However, research has found there are a number of life events that may occur throughout people's lives that usually cause a person to experience stress to some degree. The amount of stress caused by these events will vary from person to person depending on how it is viewed by them. For example, being made redundant or laid-off may be seen by one person as an opportunity to do something else with their life, whereas someone else may worry about the fact they may not be able to pay their mortgage. This could trigger clinical anxiety.

Exercise – Life Events questionnaire

Place a cross (X) in the 'Yes' column for each event which has taken place in the last two years. Then circle a number on the scale which best describes how upsetting the event crossed was to you, e.g. 10 being the most upsetting.

Event	Yes	Scale
Bought house		1 2 3 4 5 6 7 8 9 10
Sold house		1 2 3 4 5 6 7 8 9 10
Moved house		1 2 3 4 5 6 7 8 9 10
Major house renovation		1 2 3 4 5 6 7 8 9 10
Separation from a loved one		1 2 3 4 5 6 7 8 9 10
End of relationship		1 2 3 4 5 6 7 8 9 10
Got engaged		1 2 3 4 5 6 7 8 9 10
Got married		1 2 3 4 5 6 7 8 9 10
Marital or personal relationship problem		1 2 3 4 5 6 7 8 9 10
Awaiting divorce		1 2 3 4 5 6 7 8 9 10
Divorce		1 2 3 4 5 6 7 8 9 10
Child started school/nursery		1 2 3 4 5 6 7 8 9 10
Increased nursing responsibilities for elderly or sick person		1 2 3 4 5 6 7 8 9 10
Problems with relatives		1 2 3 4 5 6 7 8 9 10
Problems with friends/neighbours		1 2 3 4 5 6 7 8 9 10
Pet-related problems		1 2 3 4 5 6 7 8 9 10
Work-related problems		1 2 3 4 5 6 7 8 9 10
Change in nature of work		1 2 3 4 5 6 7 8 9 10
Threat of redundancy		1 2 3 4 5 6 7 8 9 10
Changed job		1 2 3 4 5 6 7 8 9 10
Made redundant		1 2 3 4 5 6 7 8 9 10
Unemployed		1 2 3 4 5 6 7 8 9 10
Retired		1 2 3 4 5 6 7 8 9 10
Increased or new bank loan/mortgage		1 2 3 4 5 6 7 8 9 10
Financial difficulty		1 2 3 4 5 6 7 8 9 10
Insurance problem		1 2 3 4 5 6 7 8 9 10

Event	Yes	Scale
Legal problem		1 2 3 4 5 6 7 8 9 10
Emotional or physical illness of close family or relative		1 2 3 4 5 6 7 8 9 10
Serious illness of close family or relative requiring hospitalisation		1 2 3 4 5 6 7 8 9 10
Surgical operation experienced by family member or relative		1 2 3 4 5 6 7 8 9 10
Death of partner/husband/wife		1 2 3 4 5 6 7 8 9 10
Death of family member or relative		1 2 3 4 5 6 7 8 9 10
Death of close friend		1 2 3 4 5 6 7 8 9 10
Emotional or physical illness of yourself		1 2 3 4 5 6 7 8 9 10
Serious illness requiring your own hospitalisation		1 2 3 4 5 6 7 8 9 10
Surgical operation on yourself		1 2 3 4 5 6 7 8 9 10
Pregnancy		1 2 3 4 5 6 7 8 9 10
Birth of baby		1 2 3 4 5 6 7 8 9 10
Birth of grandchild		1 2 3 4 5 6 7 8 9 10
Family member left home		1 2 3 4 5 6 7 8 9 10
Difficult relationship with children		1 2 3 4 5 6 7 8 9 10
Difficult relationship with parents		1 2 3 4 5 6 7 8 9 10

Plot your total score on the chart below:

Low stress		High stress
1	50	100

(adapted from Cooper et al., 1988)

The more of these events you have experienced in the last twenty–four months, especially if perceived as negative, and the changes that result as a consequence, can lead to an increase in stress for an individual.

Stage 2 of the model reflects the individual's perception of the pressure or demand and their appraisal of their ability to deal with it. For example, the external event does not necessarily have to be one of these life events. It could be giving a presentation or parking your car in a busy supermarket car-park. The evolutionary 'flight or fight' stress response will kick in if a person perceives any event as stressful. Often this appraisal will be processed very quickly and only one or two words may be thought such as, 'Oh no', 'Oh God', 'Oh shit', 'xxxxxxx', 'it's awful' or 'I can't'. Sometimes a person visualises a disaster occurring instead.

However, if the person believes they are able to cope with, and deal with, the event, or they perceive it as a challenge, they are less likely to experience the stress response.

If stressed, in stage 3, an individual will respond by displaying the stress responses shown in the model of stress (see Figure 2). Use the self-assessment exercise below and see whether you can recognise any of the responses.

Exercise:

Tick those you recognise in yourself. It may help to think back to the last time you felt stressed.

Behavioural signs – how did you behave?
Changes to sleep patterns (e.g. unable to get to sleep or waking early) ❑
Clenched fists ❑
Comfort eating ❑
Checking rituals ❑
Compulsive or impulsive behaviour ❑
Reduced work performance ❑
Poor time management ❑
Increased work absenteeism ❑
Increased proneness to accidents ❑
Nervous tics ❑
Procrastination ❑
Tremor in voice ❑
Grinding teeth ❑
Avoidance of situation or phobias ❑
Reduction in productivity ❑
Frequently weepy ❑

Affect and Emotional – how did you feel?
Angry ❑
Anxious ❑
Frightened, nervous or apprehensive ❑
Guilty ❑
Embarrassed or ashamed ❑
Jealous ❑
Experienced swings in mood ❑
Helpless ❑
Increased worrying ❑
Suicidal feelings ❑
Withdrawal into daydreams ❑
Depressed ❑
Unable to concentrate ❑

Sensory – what sensations were you experiencing?
Tension headaches/migraines ❑

Vague aches and pains/backaches ❏
Tremors ❏
Nausea ❏
Increased fatigue/tiredness ❏
Tightness in the chest/pains in the chest ❏
Rapid heart beat/palpitations ❏
Fainting/dizziness ❏
Indigestion ❏
Butterflies in the stomach ❏
Dry mouth/clammy hands ❏

Imagery – what were you imagining or picturing in your mind's eye?
Imagining yourself failing at the challenge ❏
Awaking early in the morning imagining yourself in a stressful situation ❏
Imagining the long-term consequences of the event ❏
Imagining the event as catastrophic ❏
Unable to put the event out of your head ❏
Images of being out of control ❏
Imagining yourself alone with nobody to help or support you ❏
Distressing dreams or nightmares ❏
Images of death or suicide ❏
Having a poor self-image ❏

Cognitive – what were your thoughts?
Unable to think of how to solve the problem ❏
Thoughts of inadequacy (e.g. 'I'm worthless and useless') ❏
Only able to think about the negative aspects ❏
Thoughts of self-blame (e.g. 'It's my fault') ❏
Believing other people will think you are stupid if unable to perform ❏
Paranoid thinking ❏
Believing life or events are 'awful' or 'unbearable' ❏
Thoughts such as 'I have to perform 100% well all the time otherwise I'm a
    failure' ❏
'I can't stand it!' ❏
Suicidal thoughts ❏

Interpersonal – how were you interacting with others?
Increased aggressive behaviour ❏
Sulking or withdrawing ❏
Being timid/shy ❏
Decreased socialising ❏
Being more argumentative/aggressive with people to whom you are close ❏
Being short-tempered or irritable ❏
Losing patience more quickly ❏
Sulking behaviour ❏
Making poor eye contact ❏
Being a loner ❏

Being over-competitive ❏
Putting the needs of others before your own ❏
Being secretive or suspicious ❏

Drug related/biological signs – how were you and your body reacting?
Increased smoking ❏
Increased caffeine consumption (tea or coffee) ❏
Increased alcohol consumption/drug abuse ❏
Breathlessness ❏
Palpitations or pounding of the heart ❏
Fainting ❏
Skin rashes and allergies ❏
Diarrhoea/constipation ❏
Excessive sweating ❏
Rapid increases or decreases in weight ❏
Changes in the menstrual cycle ❏
Reliance on drugs such as tranquillisers or alcohol ❏
High blood pressure ❏
Irritable bowel syndrome ❏
Increase in number of colds/flu ❏
Chronic fatigue/exhaustion ❏

This list can be used for self-assessment, as well as a tool to help you recognise how other people may react and behave under stress. Once you have identified which symptoms you displayed, you will be able to recognise the next time you become stressed more easily.

If you frequently experience more than five of these symptoms you may wish to seek the advice of your General Practitioner. Similarly, some of the more serious symptoms, such as frequent chest pains, fainting or suicidal thoughts, may require urgent medical attention. But do remember the checklists above are just a guide, as some of the symptoms shown may indicate a medical problem for which you may already be receiving attention.

If you experienced any of these responses when you imagined yourself in a stressful situation, you may find the next seven chapters useful. They aim to provide you with some key techniques and strategies on how to deal with these symptoms. So if you find that when stressed you become more argumentative and aggressive towards your partner you may find the section on interpersonal interventions useful; whereas if you find you binge eat and consequently put on weight, you will find the chapter on biological and drug interventions more useful.

At stage 4 of the model the person re-appraises whether or not the original situation at stage 1 of the model is still stressful. If you believe you have resolved the situation, or are at least managing it, then the stress response will usually switch off. However, it may be re-activated if the individual still negatively re-appraises the situation.

Stage 5 refers to the situation where you are unable to re-appraise the external pressure or event and therefore you still perceive it as stressful. In this instance you will continue to display some of the stress responses because you still believe you are not coping with or managing it.

Stage 6 of the model occurs if the stress response continues over a prolonged period of time resulting in more serious psychological and/or physical disorders (Leonard and Miller, 1995; Toates, 1995). This becomes a vicious circle because the very fact the individual may have developed a stress related illness may mean that they have less energy and drive to deal with the original problem. For example, their reduced performance negatively impacts upon resolving the problem; finally they are likely to perceive the illness as a further stress factor, thus perpetuating the cycle of stress. At this stage they are more likely to experience exhaustion or burnout.

Case study

John believed he was unable to meet the targets set by his manager because they were unrealistic. John did not deal with the situation with his manager, and found himself becoming increasingly aggressive. He then lost his temper in a meeting and directed all this anger and frustration at a colleague — this in turn led to an official complaint being made resulting in disciplinary action. As a result of this, John felt more angry and de-motivated and this led to him under-performing and eventually he was sacked from his company. Consequently, John became depressed; he perceived he was a 'failure' because he had lost his job. If John had dealt with the situation earlier and identified how he was going to cope with it, he may not have developed clinical depression.

Locus of control

Control is an important constituent of stress (Rotter, 1966). Researchers have found that if you believe or perceive you are in control of your life or specific situations, you will suffer from less stress, anxiety and depression (for an interesting review of this topic, see Ruiz-Bueno, 2000). The exercise opposite explores this further.

Exercise – Locus of control questionnaire

Circle the number that best reflects your attitudes

	Strongly disagree	Disagree	Uncertain	Agree	Strongly agree
Our society is run by a few people with enormous power and there is not much the ordinary person can do about it.	1	2	3	4	5
One's success is determined by 'being' in the right place at the right time.	1	2	3	4	5
There will always be industrial relations disputes no matter how hard people try to prevent them or the extent to which they try to take an active role in union activities.	1	2	3	4	5
Politicians are inherently self-interested and inflexible. It is impossible to change the course of politics.	1	2	3	4	5
What happens in life is pre-destined.	1	2	3	4	5
People are inherently lazy, so there is no point in spending too much time in changing them.	1	2	3	4	5
I do not see a direct connection between the way and how hard I work and the assessments of my performance that others arrive at.	1	2	3	4	5
Leadership qualities are primarily inherited.	1	2	3	4	5
I am fairly certain that luck and chance play a crucial role in life.	1	2	3	4	5
Even though some people try to control events by taking part in political and social affairs, in reality most of us are subject to forces we can neither comprehend nor control.	1	2	3	4	5

Plot your total score on the chart below

Internal		External
10	30	50

(Source: Cooper et al., 1988)

Interestingly, there is also a health locus of control which relates to how much we perceive we understand and can influence our health-related behaviour. In other words, taking action to deal with any problems we may be experiencing with our health. Not surprisingly, individuals who decide that they are going to take positive action regarding an illness may have better medical outcomes than those who take little action apart from just taking medication.

3

Behavioural techniques and strategies

In this chapter we look at techniques to deal with the behavioural responses to stress such as aggression or avoidance behaviour. Strategies to address behavioural responses include stability zones, time management, stimulus control, graded exposure (used to reduce specific phobias) and response prevention.

When we are stressed we often behave in unhelpful ways. Common behaviours include:

- Type A behaviour
- Procrastination
- Obsessive compulsive behaviour

This chapter will also cover these problems.

At the end of the following seven chapters is a section for you to complete regarding problems you wish to deal with and techniques you wish to use. It is important to complete these sections as it will help you develop your own action plan or profile at a later stage in this book.

Type A behaviours

People who display Type A behaviour characteristics are more prone to stress. Type A people exhibit hostile and competitive behaviour and research carried out by Drs Rosenman, Friedman and associates (1975; see also Friedman and Rosenman, 1974) showed that people with Type A behaviour had an increased risk of suffering from coronary heart disease (CHD). Type A behaviours include impatience, aggressiveness, more rapid speech and hurried behaviour. Type A people are often high achievers and competitive. In contrast Type B people are more relaxed, easygoing and patient and less likely to suffer from CHD. Many of the Type A behaviours can be dealt with by deploying the techniques and strategies explained in later chapters. For example, to manage anger more effectively, you could use time management skills (Chapter 3), relaxation techniques (Chapter 5), thinking skills (Chapter 7), or assertiveness techniques (Chapter 8).

Later research indicates that one of the main factors that may lead to CHD in people who exhibit type A behaviour is how an individual deals with their anger. For instance, people who both express and repress their anger dependent upon the situation they are trying to deal with and manage, are more likely to increase the chances of suffering from coronary heart disease. Therefore it would be better not to become so wound up in the first instance.

Exercise – Type A questionnaire

Use this exercise to determine whether you are more Type A or B. Circle one number for each of the statements below which best reflects the way you behave in your everyday life. For example, if you are generally on time for appointments, for the first point you would circle a number between 7 and 11. If you usually casual about appointments you would circle one of the lower numbers between 1 and 5.

Casual about appointments	1 2 3 4 5 6 7 8 9 10 11	Never late
Non competitive	1 2 3 4 5 6 7 8 9 10 11	Very competitive
Good listener	1 2 3 4 5 6 7 8 9 10 11	Anticipates what others are going to say (nods, attempts to finish for them)
Never feels rushed (even under pressure)	1 2 3 4 5 6 7 8 9 10 11	Always rushed
Can wait patiently	1 2 3 4 5 6 7 8 9 10 11	Impatient while waiting
Takes things one at a time	1 2 3 4 5 6 7 8 9 10 11	Tries to do many things at once, thinks about what will do next
Slow deliberate talker	1 2 3 4 5 6 7 8 9 10 11	Emphatic in speech, fast and forceful
Cares about satisfying him/ herself no matter what others think	1 2 3 4 5 6 7 8 9 10 11	Wants good job recognised by others
Slow doing things	1 2 3 4 5 6 7 8 9 10 11	Fast (eating, walking)
Easy-going	1 2 3 4 5 6 7 8 9 10 11	Hard driving (pushing yourself and others)
Expresses feelings	1 2 3 4 5 6 7 8 9 10 11	Hides feelings
Many outside interests	1 2 3 4 5 6 7 8 9 10 11	Few interests outside work/home
Unambitious	1 2 3 4 5 6 7 8 9 10 11	Ambitious
Casual	1 2 3 4 5 6 7 8 9 10 11	Eager to get things done

Plot score below:

Type B		Type A
14	84	154

(Source: Cooper's adaptation of The Bortner Type A Scale, 1969, Cooper et al., 1988.)

Now you have completed the exercise, how Type A are you? If you have any situations that have high Type A scores which often trigger stress and/or anger, consider how you can reduce your stress levels. For example, apart from avoiding the situations, consider how could you learn to wait patiently? Note down below what you want to do.

_____

_____

_____

_____

Overcoming procrastination

Think back to a time when you had to study for an exam or complete an important project either at work or in the house. Did you engage in time-wasting activities that were not actually going to help you to complete your project? If so, you were procrastinating. A section on procrastination is included in the chapter on stress and studying (Chapter 12).

The problem with procrastination is that in the long run it increases stress. When we want to do a task well, our stress levels often increase. Engaging in unimportant behaviours causes a drop in our stress levels – a quick fix! However, the drop is only temporary because later when you focus on the real task in hand that you are trying to avoid, your stress levels rise even higher in the realisation you have wasted yet more time. The key is to spot if you find yourself performing an action that is not directly focused on helping you to achieve the task or goal. Examples include cleaning, tidying up files, surfing the internet, deleting unimportant emails, drinking, smoking, comfort eating, whinging to friends and colleagues and so on.

Obsessive-compulsive behaviour

Obsessions can be defined as recurrent thoughts, impulses or images which occur involuntarily. Compulsions are repetitive, voluntary, and purposeless aspects of behaviour carried out according to a set of rules held in the mind of the individual. When a person suffering from obsessive-compulsive disorder behaves accordingly, it will usually lower their level of anxiety. For example, touching the door handle a specific number of times in order to ensure a 'feared' event will not occur. Compulsive rituals with obsessions include checking, cleaning, orderliness, hoarding and repeating (Marks, 1980). When a person is stressed an otherwise 'normal' behaviour may become exaggerated if the person is feeling particularly anxious and lead to obsessive-compulsive behaviours such as excessive hand-washing or checking. Response prevention (see page 25) may help reduce obsessive-compulsive behaviours. A referral to a psychologist or cognitive-behavioural therapist may be necessary if the condition is distressing.

Techniques and strategies

Behavioural rehearsal

If you want to act in a desired manner such as become assertive or improve your presentation skills, one of the best methods is to gain as much practice as possible. This can be undertaken in the comfort of your home or in a quiet room at work. Think about what you want to do, note down the actions involved and what you want to say. Then practise, practise, practise, out aloud, imagining you have the particular person or audience in front of you.

Case study

Laura experienced stress and anxiety whenever she had to give her opinion at the weekly general office meeting. She would start to stammer and become embarrassed. Usually, she spent the entire week trying not to think about this regular Friday event. This maintained her high stress levels as she avoided preparing for the meeting and understandably, became anxious about what she should say. On Wednesday evening at home, she noted down her opinion regarding the new computer programme which had been recently installed at work. She summarised her thoughts into one concise paragraph. Then she sat in front of a mirror and repeated the paragraph 20 times until she became familiar with it. She noted that if she simultaneously slowly breathed out and read aloud, she was far less likely to stammer. (This was an

---

important insight.) She adjusted one sentence slightly as it was not easy to say aloud. She repeated this exercise on Thursday evening recording her voice on a cassette recorder. On replaying the tape, she noticed that she sounded reasonably relaxed. On Friday, at the meeting, as soon as the problem of the new computer programme was raised she took the opportunity to state her view. Although she was still slightly nervous, she felt more confident and was pleased with the outcome.

Stability zones and routines

Stability zones can be thought of as those physical areas where a person may be able to relax, feel safe and forget about their worries (Palmer, 1989). These may be different for every individual but some examples may include the park, room, bath, beach, holiday home, or caravan. Routines are enjoyable regular or irregular habits such as walking the dog, morning cup of coffee, weekend breaks, holidays, playing a musical instrument, watching favourite films or television programmes, reading a book or newspaper on the journey into work. Stability zones are can also be intrinsically linked with a routine, for example, drinking a cup of tea whilst sitting in your favourite chair. Stability zones and routines are one way of coping with stress and pressure. They act as a stress buffer when used in moderation.

Exercise

Note down below your stability zones and routines.

_____

_____

_____

_____

Are there any you have given up due to pressure of work or life events? Consider whether you wish to start using them again to help you relax.

Time Management

If you are managing your time effectively, you are likely to feel in control and more able to reduce your stress both at home and work.

However, often when we feel stressed, we manage our time less efficiently and effectively. This only exaggerates the feelings of being out of control, thus increasing our levels of stress. Time management techniques are a useful way to deal with procrastination.

Time management tips

1. At the start of the week, make a list of your goals and what you would like to achieve. Prioritise the list. Revise it daily or as necessary. Regularly refer to the list.

2. Only spend an appropriate amount of time planning your workload or project.

3. Avoid procrastinating. Challenge what is underpinning this behaviour.

4. Do one task at a time to avoid making errors.

5. Allow time for the unexpected and be realistic about how much you can achieve.

6. Avoid automatically saying 'yes' to others' requests. Ask yourself what the consequences will be if you say 'no' to the request.

7. If at work, deal with incoming emails and post as soon as you open them. If under pressure, prioritise them. Group outgoing calls together and list what you need to discuss in order to keep the calls precise and brief.

Exercise

Below is a quick exercise to enable you to measure how much of your time you utilise to your satisfaction. You will need a large piece of paper and a pen or pencil.

Draw two large circles on the paper.

Make a list of all the activities you do in an average week. For example, eating, sleeping, cooking, working, attending classes, looking after children, reading, seeing friends etc.

Divide the first circle up into segments to represent the amount of time you spend on each of these activities. It will look like a pie chart.

In the second circle, segment it in the same way. However, this time focus on the amount of satisfaction you gain from each activity. For example, you may believe you gain less satisfaction from being at work, than you do visiting friends. In this case, seeing friends will represent a larger portion of the chart.

This simple exercise will help you to consider all aspects of your life by making you more aware of the amount of time you dedicate to activities that provide you with satisfaction and therefore less stress.

Stimulus control

Individuals may increase or decrease specific behaviours in the presence of certain stimuli. For example, smokers may be more likely to smoke when in a pub or bar with friends. If smokers wish to reduce the number of cigarettes they smoke they could use stimulus control. In this instance, the approach may involve the individual only smoking at a specific time of the day, or in a particular chair at home. Other examples may include comfort eating when feeling stressed. If you find yourself doing this, limit the number of snacks available in the house or office, and instead buy healthier options such as fruit.

Graded behavioural exposure

This technique is frequently used to overcome specific phobias. Through our experience, we have found this behavioural approach can stop lifetime phobias in one or two therapy sessions. With mild cases, people can often overcome their phobias without professional assistance. It works on the principle of exposing the individual to the real life stimuli about which they are phobic such as spiders or travelling on crowded trains. When the person has remained in contact with, or in the presence of the feared situation for some time, their anxiety levels begin to reduce and eventually habituate (return to normal). The procedure is no different to the advice given to a rider who has fallen off a horse or bicycle; unless they are injured they are instructed to 'Get back on'.

Exposure is usually graded in discrete steps so as not to expose the individual to the most feared situation immediately. This process can be aided by ranking your fears in a hierarchical order and representing the level of distress and anxiety each triggers on a scale of 0–10 where 0 represents no anxiety and 10 represents high levels of anxiety and panic.

Case study

Emma was about to start a new job. She was really excited about it. However, the new job required her to commute by train which triggered high levels of anxiety. It was no longer feasible for her to drive to work. Emma drew up her hierarchy of fears on a scale of 0–10 where 0 represented no anxiety and 10 represented extremely high levels of anxiety and panic.

Rank	Scale of fear	Event
1	10	Standing in a crowded train
2	8	Sitting in a crowded train
3	6	Standing in an un-crowded train
4	5	Sitting in an un-crowded train
5	4.5	Buying a ticket for a train journey

Emma decided to confront her fear by exposing herself to each of these events in turn. Emma first taught herself relaxation techniques (explained later in Chapter 5) in order to manage her anxiety levels. Each time she confronted an event she noted in her diary, her anxiety levels before, during and after the event. She also noted how she felt and the coping strategies she used to overcome each event, such as monitoring her breathing to relax. Eventually over a period of about four weeks she was able to confront all the events in the hierarchy of fears, and travel to her new job on a crowded train.

Other helpful techniques involve imagining yourself in the feared situation. Imaginal exposure and coping imagery are described in more detail in Chapter 6. These techniques are particularly useful if you believe you cannot face the feared object initially.

If you are keen to find out more about this graded exposure technique you may like to seek the help and support of a behavioural therapist or psychologist who will practise this approach.

Response cost

This strategy helps to discourage a person from undertaking any unwanted behaviour and focus on a new desired behaviour (Marks, 1986). For example, if you wish to stop smoking or lose weight, you can contract with a friend to donate to a charity a sum of money whenever you smoke or eat unhealthy food. Sometimes this cost or penalty is not enough. Better still make a donation to your least favourite mainstream political party or charity. This really encourages some people to change their unwanted behaviour!

Response prevention

Response prevention is a technique used to help reduce or stop obsessive-compulsive behaviour. By exposing the person to the ritual evoking cues such as a dirty kitchen surface or negative thoughts and *not* carrying out the ritualistic anxiety-reducing behaviour such as hand washing, touching an object, or whatever, eventually the anxiety subsides (Marks, 1980; 1986). Therefore a person who hand washes excessively after touching a 'contaminated' item attempts to delay the time between this event and when they finally wash their hands. A person who has the compulsion to touch an object such as a door handle twenty times when they feel anxious will attempt not to touch it for as long as possible. If they do touch it, they attempt to touch it less times, say fifteen times. With practice, gradually the person becomes less anxious about not undertaking their ritualistic behaviour.

Self-assessment

It is useful to assess the strategies that you apply to deal with stress.

Exercise

Coping with life stress questionnaire

(adapted from Cooper et al., 1988)

The purpose of this questionnaire is to find out how people deal with situations, which trouble them.

Take a few moments and think about an event or situation, which has been most stressful to you. By 'stressful' we mean a serious situation, which was difficult, troubling or upsetting to you. It might have been something to do with your family, your friends, your spouse or children.

Thinking about the situation, to what extent do you do the following?

	Never	Rarely	Periodically	Regularly	Very often
Temporary Adaptation Part 1					
Get on with work, keep busy	1	2	3	4	5
Throw yourself into work	1	2	3	4	5
Do some housework	1	2	3	4	5
Try to do something where you don't use your mind	1	2	3	4	5
Cry on your own	1	2	3	4	5
Bottle it up for a time, then break down	1	2	3	4	5
Explosive, mostly temper, not tears	1	2	3	4	5
Treat yourself to something, e.g. clothes, meals out	1	2	3	4	5
Helpful behaviour Part 2					
Sit and think	1	2	3	4	5
Ability to cry with friends	1	2	3	4	5
Get angry with people or things which cause the problem	1	2	3	4	5
Let feelings out, talk to close friends	1	2	3	4	5
Talk things over with lots of friends	1	2	3	4	5
Go over the problem again and again in your mind to try to understand it	1	2	3	4	5
Feel you learn something from every distress	1	2	3	4	5
Talk to someone who could do something about the problem	1	2	3	4	5
Try to get sympathy and understanding from someone	1	2	3	4	5
Unhelpful behaviour Part 3					
Try not to think about it	5	4	3	2	1
Go quiet	5	4	3	2	1
Go on as if nothing happened	5	4	3	2	1
Keep feelings to yourself	5	4	3	2	1
Avoid being with people	5	4	3	2	1
Show a 'brave face'	5	4	3	2	1
Worry constantly	5	4	3	2	1
Lose sleep	5	4	3	2	1
Don't eat	5	4	3	2	1
Control tears (hide feelings)	5	4	3	2	1
Eat more	5	4	3	2	1
Wish that you could change what happened	5	4	3	2	1
Have fantasies or wishes about how things might have turned out	5	4	3	2	1

Plot total score below:

Unhelpful _____ Helpful

29   87   145

Now you have completed the questionnaire, decide what you could do to increase your overall score. In particular, focus on actions that will help you raise the scores in parts 2 and 3 of the questionnaire. (Part 1 behaviours although maybe helpful in the short term, are not always so helpful with long standing problems.) Note down the items that you want to change. Consider how you may go about taking a different approach to dealing with stress provoking problems.

Conclusion

Many of the behavioural responses can also be dealt with and addressed through the techniques and strategies discussed in later chapters. For instance, aggressive, Type A behaviour can be dealt with by understanding your unhelpful thoughts that may be making you behave in that way, and using thinking skills to challenge them. Similarly, relaxation exercises or massage may help to reduce behaviours such as nervous tics or teeth grinding.

Exercise

Now you have finished this chapter, please complete the section below.
What problems do you wish to resolve or manage?

What techniques or strategies do you wish to use to help you deal with the problems noted above?

4
Emotional techniques and strategies

This chapter focuses on the recognition of, and dealing with, the troublesome emotional feelings experienced under stress. It is important to remember that these feelings are intrinsically associated with our behaviours, thoughts and images. So techniques described in Chapters 3, 6 and 7 will also be of use. Before reading the techniques and strategies to deal with the emotional response to stress, try the exercise below.

Exercise

Think back to the last time you felt guilty about the way you behaved or spoke to someone, or were very angry. As you attempt to feel angry or guilty try to experience the feelings without having a thought or a picture in your mind.

It is not easy to do is it? Is it possible to have or experience that emotion without also having a thought in your head, or visualising some sort of image?

For example, if you are feeling very angry about the way your manager is expecting you to do more and more work, and yet still answer his or her phone all day, it may help to examine if there are any negative thoughts which are contributing to this stress. Are you reducing your tolerance to the situation by telling yourself 'I can't stand it'?

Or are you inferring things about the future consequences without any evidence? For example, are you convincing yourself that your manager will sack you if you do not complete all the work, even though this has never been said to you?

These sorts of negative thoughts are known as thinking errors and are explained in more detail in the section on cognitive interventions (Chapter 7). The interventions include how to use thinking skills to alleviate the negative or irrational thoughts. Another way of addressing this anger would be to arrange a meeting with your manager and explain you have too much to do. List the activities that you can achieve and those which either need to cease or be done by another person. You could also suggest your manager uses a voicemail facility meaning you will not be in the position where you feel obliged constantly to answer the phone.

The exercise demonstrates how many of your emotional responses to stress cannot be completely isolated from the other responses to stress. However, feeling identification, emotion management and even medication are useful methods to manage your emotions when under stress.

Helpful versus unhelpful troublesome emotions

It is important to identify what emotions you are feeling when under stress. Some emotions are more helpful in a crisis. For example, feeling very anxious about meeting a deadline may lead to procrastination and time wasting such as unnecessary tidying of office files and surfing the internet, whereas feeling concerned may help you to focus on your goal. Feeling depressed about losing your job may lead to withdrawal and not applying for other posts, whereas when you feel sad you accept the situation but may still be motivated to apply for new jobs.

It is unlikely in a stressful situation that you will not suffer from an emotion. Feeling nothing will be unrealistic! Below is a table of helpful and unhelpful emotions.

Table 4.1 Healthy and unhealthy troublesome negative emotions and their correlating thoughts (Palmer & Dryden, 1995)

Inference related to personal domain	Type of belief	Emotion
Threat or danger	Unhelpful	Anxiety
Threat or danger	Helpful	Concern
Loss (with implications for future); failure	Unhelpful	Depression
Loss (with implications for future); failure	Helpful	Sadness
Breaking of own moral code	Unhelpful	Guilt
Breaking of own moral code	Helpful	Remorse
Breaking of personal rule (other or self); other threatens self; frustration	Unhelpful	Damning anger
Breaking of personal rule (other or self); other threatens self; frustration	Helpful	Non-damning anger (or annoyance)
Personal weakness revealed publicly	Unhelpful	Shame/ embarrassment

Inference related to personal domain	Type of belief	Emotion
Personal weakness revealed publicly	Helpful	Regret
Other betrays self (self non-deserving)	Unhelpful	Hurt
Other betrays self (self non-deserving)	Helpful	Disappointment
Threat to desired exclusive relationship	Unhelpful	Morbid jealousy
Threat to desired exclusive relationship	Helpful	Non-morbid jealousy

Exercise

Use the space below to note any emotions you feel when stressed and identify whether they are helpful or unhelpful. In other words, do they help you to achieve your goal(s)?

_____

_____

_____

_____

_____

_____

_____

Which troublesome emotions would you like to work on? Think about how you can tackle them the next time they arise. Note down the unhelpful and stress-inducing images and thoughts that are associated with them. Chapters 6 and 7 will help you modify these.

Feeling identification

You can use Table 4.1 above to help you identify what emotions you experience when under stress. However the following case study and exercise will also help you.

Case study

Peter does not enjoy giving presentations. He feels anxious beforehand and during the event the anxiety he feels actually reduces his ability to deliver the speech. For example, his throat and mouth become dry, talking becomes difficult and his voice becomes squeaky and high-pitched. He experiences butterflies in his stomach and his hands become sweaty and clammy, making it harder to move from one page of his notes to the next. In other words, Peter's anxiety response reduces his performance in delivering the presentation.

Exercise

In order to identify the emotions you experience when under stress, ask yourself the questions below and look at Table 4.1, which explains the relationship between helpful and unhelpful emotions, and their correlating helpful or unhelpful beliefs.

Questions;
What do you get angry about?
What do you get anxious about?
What do you get sad about?
Do you have a persistent recurring negative emotion?
How do your emotions affect your relationships?

Emotional expression – The empty chair technique

If you repress your emotions (such as anger or jealousy) you may find this method useful to help release them and deal with them appropriately. It is known as the 'empty chair' technique and can also be an interpersonal strategy. It involves sitting yourself opposite an empty chair and imagining yourself talking to a person sitting in the other chair with whom you wish to hold a conversation. For example, if you feel angry about an appraisal your manager has given you, at your next meeting with him or her, instead of assertively discussing the relevant issues, you may become damningly angry and state what you think in an unconstructive manner, losing sight of your goals. Try the exercise overleaf using this format.

Exercise

Find a quiet room where you will not be disturbed. Sit comfortably on a chair and place an empty chair opposite you. Think of a conversation you would like to have with someone with whom you have some unfinished business. Try to say exactly what you think and feel. Do note that although it may be acceptable to criticise their behaviour it is important to avoid criticising them globally, for example, 'I don't agree with your negative comments', instead of 'I think you're crap'. You may sit in the other chair at any point during your conversation and if it will help you, respond in the usual manner of the other person. Continue going back and forth with the discussion until you gain a resolution or believe you have made an insight into your differences.

Case study

Karen was angry about the way her neighbour, David, had cut back the trees in their garden and had damaged the adjoining fence with Karen's own garden. Karen knew David was not particularly thoughtful about other people and tended to do exactly what he wanted with no regard for anyone living locally. Karen was not very good at expressing anger and tended to repress her emotions rather than cause a scene. However, this was not the first time David had damaged Karen's property. This time she felt she had to confront him. Karen first decided to practise using the 'empty chair' technique. She sat down and expressed her damning anger: 'I really hate you. You are always treating me badly. You're useless'. She sat in the other chair and considered how she thought David would reply: 'It's my garden and I can do what I want. You are taking this too personally and I'm not prepared to talk to you.' At this stage, Karen had expressed how she felt, but realised taking this approach was not going to help her resolve the situation. Karen reflected on a different approach. She returned to her chair and went on to explain how she would appreciate David paying to replace the broken fence. The conversation continued with Karen explaining why she felt angry, especially as David behaved in a selfish manner. Although this debate was not resolving the situation, Karen realised if she continued with this technique she would eventually find a solution. Karen decided to offer David a compromise: 'Either you pay for the damage or I will contact the insurance company. The choice is yours'. David insisted on saying nothing more so Karen left saying: 'I'll be in touch with the insurance company first thing in the morning' and left David.

> By playing out the role-play, Karen felt better because she had run through a way to deal with a difficult situation that she would normally avoid. It also enabled Karen actually to talk to David and co-operate with him because she no longer felt damningly angry, only annoyed.

Anger management

Do you find yourself becoming very angry if you have to wait for a delayed train, or are stuck in a traffic jam, or are not able to use the video recorder properly? If so, you may find this anger management technique useful.

Exercise

1. Note down your thoughts when you feel angry about a situation (like being stuck in a traffic jam).
2. Note down any pictures or images when you feel angry.
3. Note down your behaviours (do you raise your voice, bang your fist on the dash-board of the car?)
4. Notice how your body feels. Do you feel hotter? Is your heart beating faster?
5. For different responses you may need to apply different techniques explained in other chapters. For example, use the strategies explained in Chapter 6 to modify negative images or pictures, Chapter 7 to deal with your thoughts, use Chapter 3 to address your behavioural responses, Chapter 5 to help you relax and Chapter 8 to learn assertiveness skills.
6. Develop an action plan to refer back to when you feel angry. This can be used again next time you find yourself in the situation about which you tend to feel angry.

Anxiety management

Anxiety and anger are the two key emotions involved with stress. As with anger management, anxiety levels can be reduced by employing a range of interventions that are explained in the rest of the book.

For example, individuals can experience anxiety, triggered by a number of situations; travelling on a plane, driving a vehicle, giving a presentation or wedding speech. Anxiety can be dealt with by using thinking skills, facing your fear, using relaxation or imagery techniques, being assertive with your family, friends or work colleagues or medication.

Medication to deal with depression and anxiety

The use of medication is another way to deal with emotions such as anxiety and depression. Any drugs of this kind need to be prescribed by a medical practitioner and used with care as they may have strong side effects. If you are feeling depressed or anxious, it would be advisable to visit your GP for advice and perhaps a referral to a counsellor, psychiatrist or psychologist. It is important to remember that it is not a sign of weakness if you need to take medication.

Conclusion

Troublesome emotions do not usually appear 'out of the blue'. Often events may trigger negative thoughts and images that influence how we feel emotionally. For example, to feel guilty about an action we may have undertaken, we are probably telling ourselves, 'I should not have done it'. These thoughts are largely responsible for us feeling guilty. Similarly, to feel damningly angry about our partner's behaviour, we may be telling ourselves, 'He is a total failure. He shouldn't have forgotten to pick me up at the station'. In Chapter 7, we consider how to modify our thinking to help us feel and act in more helpful ways.

Exercise

Now you have finished this chapter, please complete the section below.

What problems do you wish to resolve or manage?

What techniques or strategies do you wish to use to help you deal with the problems noted above?

5
Sensory techniques and strategies

The strategies outlined in this chapter will help to deal with your sensory responses to stress such as butterflies in the stomach, tension headaches, palpitations and general aches and pains. Many of the techniques explained can be used in conjunction with other interventions, such as imagery exercises or thinking skills (described in Chapters 6 and 7 respectively). The sensory methods include relaxation, massage and biofeedback.

Relaxation

Relaxation is a word we have all heard, but few people know how to use relaxation techniques. Indeed many of us do not use these techniques because we relax in other ways. Recent research found the main method people used to relax was watching television (Palmer, 2000). Other people relax by smoking or drinking alcohol, and the negative impacts of these methods of 'relaxation' are discussed in more detail in Chapter 9. Many people also find reading, having a bath or listening to music useful ways to relax. If you find these relax you (apart from smoking or drinking), there is no reason why you should not continue to use them (see Stability zones and routines, page 21).

The relaxation methods described below have been found to be useful by many thousands of people to alleviate the physical effects of stress and tension. The techniques focus on switching off the sympathetic nervous system which is your stress or arousal response, and stimulating the parasympathetic nervous system that is responsible for relaxation and conserving your body's energy levels.

Below are two relaxation exercises (Benson, 1976; Palmer, 1993). During the exercises you may experience odd sensations such as tingling or warmth in your hands or light-headedness. If you do not like these feelings simply open your eyes and they will pass away quickly.

Benson relaxation technique (Benson, 1976)

This Western form of relaxation has been found to reduce hypertension and high blood pressure. It involves using a number of your choice, frequently the number one, as a mantra. Focusing on this helps to ignore any unwanted, negative or intrusive thoughts. With this technique there are a number of stages to follow.

Exercise

1. Find a place where there is as little noise as possible, and you will not be disturbed.
2. Either lie or sit in a comfortable position.
3. Close your eyes.
4. Relax your muscles in groups, starting with your face and moving down to your toes. This can be done by first tensing or squeezing a muscle, and then relaxing it.
5. Focus on your breathing. Breathe in through your nose and out through your mouth. Avoid raising your shoulders as you breathe. Imagine you are breathing from your stomach, and notice how it may rise and fall as you breathe.
6. In your mind say a number every time you breathe out such as number 'one'.
7. Continue doing this for 5–20 minutes.
8. Finish in your own time. When you feel ready to stop, keep your eyes closed and sit or lie quietly for a few minutes.

If you find you are being distracted by other thoughts, let them pass and go back to repeating your chosen number. The important rule about relaxation is not to try too hard. With regular practice you will find relaxation comes to you naturally, but it may take a while before this happens.

Biofeedback

A good way to measure your stress levels is to measure the biological functions of the body.

There are a number of instruments or measuring devices that can be purchased. They can measure blood pressure, heart rate or skin electrical conductivity or temperature. As these instruments provide feedback to the observer on the biological responses of the body, they are known as 'biofeedback' instruments.

Blood pressure machines are available to purchase and measure your heart rate and blood pressure both of which increase when you are stressed, aroused or exerting yourself.

Your skin temperature also changes as part of the stress response. When you relax the small blood capillaries near the skin dilate and the blood flow therefore increases – this causes a rise in the temperature. However, when you are stressed the blood is directed away from where it is not needed such as your digestive system and the capillaries near the surface of your skin, to your key organs such as the heart and major muscles. This reduces the temperature of your hands and feet.

Biodots are a practical and cheap biofeedback method to measure this response. They are small dots (about 4 mm in diameter) that are placed on your skin and they change colour depending on your skin temperature. Biodots can be purchased through the Centre for Stress Management, London, UK (see Appendix on page 136).

At the same time when you become stressed or aroused you begin to sweat within 1–2 seconds (this increases the electrical conductivity of the skin). A galvanic skin response (GSR) monitor can be used to measure changing skin conductivity. The GSR can respond either by a change in audio tone or a movement on a monitor.

Hypnosis
For over a century, hypnosis has been used to help people to deal with stress and a range of physical conditions such as headaches, migraines, irritable bowel syndrome, phobias, skin disorders, smoking, reducing blushing, tension, pain management and over eating. Essentially, hypnosis works by helping a person to relax (Palmer, 1993). As this occurs they become more receptive to positive or helpful statements made by a therapist or included on a self-help audio tape. There is a list of organisations that hold a register of qualified practitioners in the Appendix.

Multimodal relaxation technique (Palmer, 1993)
The Multimodal Relaxation Method was developed by Professor Stephen Palmer at the Centre for Stress Management to help clients attending counselling sessions and delegates attending stress management workshops to find the particular technique that suits them. It contains a number of different strategies including breathing, mantras, imagery, sounds,

smell and touch (Palmer, 1993). Once you have tried the method, decide which strategy you prefer for future use.

Below is the Multimodal Relaxation Method script that you can either ask someone to read to you, or record yourself reading so you can play it back later. Obviously, do not read out aloud the instructions to pause!

(NB If you wear contact lenses either remove them before the exercise or do not look upwards. A long pause is about 10 seconds.)

Multimodal Relaxation Manuscript

Begin by sitting comfortably on a chair and close your eyes. If at any time during the exercise you feel any odd feelings such as tingling sensations, light-headedness, or whatever, this is quite normal. If you open your eyes then these feelings will go away. If you carry on with the exercise usually these feelings will disappear anyway.

If you would like to listen to the noises outside the room first of all
Long pause
And now listen to the noises inside the room
Pause
You may be aware of yourself breathing.
These noises will come and go throughout this session and you can choose to let them just drift over your mind or ignore them if you wish
Pause
Now keeping your eyelids closed and without moving your head, I would like you to look upwards, your eyes closed, just look upwards
Long pause
Notice the feeling of tiredness
Pause
And relaxation
Pause
In your eye muscles
Pause
Now let your eyes drop back down
Pause
Notice the tiredness and relaxation in those muscles of your eyes
Pause
Let the feeling now travel down your face to your jaw, just relax your jaw
Long pause
Now relax your tongue

Pause

Let the feeling of relaxation slowly travel up over your face to the top of your head

Pause

To the back of your head

Long pause

Then slowly down through your neck muscles

Pause

And down to your shoulders

Long pause

Now concentrate on relaxing your shoulders, just let them drop down

Pause

Now let that feeling of relaxation now in your shoulders slowly travel down your right arm, down through the muscles, down through your elbow, down through your wrist, to your hand, right down to your finger tips

Long pause

Let the feeling of relaxation now in your shoulders slowly travel down your left arm, down through your muscles, down through your elbow, through your wrist, down to your hand, right down to your finger tips

Long pause

And let that feeling of relaxation now in your shoulders slowly travel down your chest right down to your stomach

Pause

Just concentrate on your breathing

Pause

Notice that every time you breathe out you feel more

Pause

And more relaxed

Long pause

Let the feeling of relaxation travel down from your shoulders right down your back

Long pause

Right down your right leg, down through the muscles, through your knee, down through your ankle

Pause

To your foot, right down to your toes

Long pause

Let the feeling of relaxation now travel down your left leg

Pause

Down through the muscles, down through your knee, down through your ankle

Pause

To your foot, right down to your toes

Long pause

I'll give you a few moments now

Pause

To allow you concentrate on any part of your body that you would like to relax further

15-second pause minimum

I want you to concentrate on your breathing again

Pause

Notice as you breathe

Pause

On each out-breath you feel more and more relaxed

Long pause

I would like you in your mind to say a number of your choice such as the number 'one'

Pause (NB If the number evokes an emotion in you choose another number)

And say it every time you breathe out

Long pause

This will help you to push away any unwanted thoughts you may have

Pause

Each time you breathe out just say the number in your mind

30-second pause

I want you now

Pause

To think of your favourite relaxing place

Long pause

Try and see it in your mind's eye

Long pause

Look at the colours

Long pause

Now focus on one colour

Long pause

Now concentrate on any sounds or noises in your favourite relaxing place. If there are no sounds, then focus on the silence

Long pause

Now concentrate on any smells or aromas in your favourite relaxing place

Long pause

Now just imagine touching something

Pause

In your favourite relaxing place

Long pause

Just imagine how it feels

Long pause

I want you now to concentrate on your breathing again

Pause

Notice once again that every time you breathe out

Pause

You feel more

Pause

And more relaxed

Long pause

Whenever you want to in the future you will be able to remember your favourite place or the breathing exercise and it will help you to relax quickly

Long pause

In a few moments' time, but not quite yet, I'm going to count to three

Pause

And you will be able to open your eyes in your own time

Pause (NB Or insert, 'go off to sleep', if you so wish)

One

Pause

Two

Pause

Three

Pause

Open your eyes in your own time

In our experience, we have found this multimodal method of relaxation to be particularly useful for people suffering from anxiety, tension headaches, high blood pressure, insomnia, Type A behaviour, and control general irritability experienced by someone on a stop smoking programme. However, care should be taken if you suffer from asthma, epilepsy or panic attacks because relaxation can exacerbate or trigger these conditions in rare cases.

If you are interested in finding out more about relaxation, yoga or meditation, you might like to contact your local adult education service which may run classes. Alternatively, a local sports centre may run classes.

© Palmer, 1993

Massage

Massage is another way directly to relieve the symptoms of aches and pains or tension headaches. In reality, we massage ourselves virtually every day. Every time you wash your hair, you are massaging your scalp. If a child bumps into an object the parent will frequently rub the painful area.

The healing powers of massage have been documented over many years including the development of techniques such as aromatherapy (the use of scented oils), reflexology, shiatsu, and Swedish massage.

The principle of massage is to apply rhythmical pressure of varying degrees to the body. The gentle pulling and stroking movements actually increase the circulation of blood to a particular area by causing the small blood vessels to dilate. The dilation of the vessels causes the body to feel warm and less tense. There are a number of types of nerve cell, but when we rub a part of our body the cells responsible for warmth are stimulated and temporarily override the slower nerve cells responsible for detecting pain. So the parent instructing a child who has hurt herself: 'Rub it better', is actually stimulating a biological reaction.

The main relaxation movements used are (Geddes & Grosset, 1999):

- Stroking or effleurage – a slow and rhythmical movement, using the whole hand in an upward direction towards the heart. A lighter, more gliding motion is used when working away from the heart. This relaxes the nervous system and increases blood circulation.
- Kneading – this movement is most suitable for unlocking tense or aching muscles especially between the neck and shoulders. Using both hands in a rhythmic sequence, gently pick up and squeeze tense muscles. This stimulates the lymphatic system and removes a build-up of lactic acid (which causes the muscle to ache).
- Friction – these strokes can be used to penetrate deep muscle tissue. Either the heel of the hands or the finger-tips and thumb are used in a circular or linear movement. Thumb pressure is very effective in releasing knotted muscles.

To find out more about massage or a specific form of it, you would be advised to attend a course or read further on the subject.

Conclusion

Sensory techniques and strategies help us to reduce physical tension. As we become less tense, we start to feel more physically relaxed as we stimulate the parasympathetic nervous system. This has the additional benefit of enhancing our immune system. Relaxation and meditation techniques have been shown to reduce blood pressure and in some cases, tackle hypertension. Thus daily relaxation exercises may be a useful addition to any stress management action plan you are developing.

Exercise

Now you have finished this chapter, please complete the section below.

What problems do you wish to resolve or manage?

What techniques or strategies do you wish to use to help you deal with the problems noted above?

6

Imagery techniques and strategies

The techniques and strategies described in this chapter will help to deal with the imagery responses to stress such as the negative mental pictures many people have in their heads when under stress. These images can serve to increase the stress or anxiety being felt. In many circumstances you hold a picture in your head of being unable to cope with a situation.

For example, you might be thinking about a presentation you are due to give, but also holding a picture of yourself in your head standing in front of the audience and being unable to deliver the speech. By holding these negative pictures in your mind you are likely to feel even more anxious and stressed about giving the presentation and increase the chances of actually giving a poor presentation. It may become a self-fulfilling prophecy.

Using imagery exercises can help to deal with these negative images you hold in your head or develop new helpful images. The common approaches include: coping imagery, motivation imagery and time projection imagery. The chapter also includes a relaxation technique using imagery and a method to deal with phobias called imaginal exposure.

Exercise

Try an example for yourself – think of an occasion when you felt stressed and picture that situation in your head. Does holding the negative picture in your head make you feel more or less stressed?

Coping imagery

This technique involves imagining yourself coping with the situation you are feeling stressed about and challenging the catastrophic or negative imagery that is winding you up. It is important to note this is called 'coping imagery' not mastery imagery, whereby you imagine yourself completing the task perfectly (McMullin, 1986). Most people who are feeling stressed about a situation, do not have the confidence to believe they will ever be able to 'master' the situation – however, it is possible to imagine themselves coping because this allows for an element of fallibility.

For example, accepting you will be able to give a perfect presentation is unlikely, but giving a presentation that is acceptable is much more believable. Using this technique can also help to deal with phobias, for example, imagining yourself coping in a full lift (claustrophobia) or sitting in a room with a spider in the corner (arachnophobia). In our experience, we have been able to treat lifetime phobias in one or two sessions.

Coping imagery exercise

There are five steps in this exercise

1. Think of the future event you are feeling stressed or anxious about.

2. Write down the particular aspects of this situation that you are feeling most stressed about.

3. Think of ways to overcome these problems – it may be useful to speak with a friend or colleague if you are unable to think of a way to deal with the problem.

4. Visualise yourself in the situation that you fear, and using the strategies you have identified in step three, slowly imagine yourself coping. Visualise yourself dealing with the problems as they arise. You may need to repeat this procedure three or four times.

5. Practise this technique regularly, especially when you find yourself feeling stressed about a situation or event.

Case study

Robert was due to deliver a presentation next week. He kept finding himself imagining standing in front of the audience with his mind going blank and not being able to speak. He decided to use coping imagery. He first visualised himself preparing the presentation and writing his prompt notes on postcards.

He then imagined himself turning up an hour before to check the overhead projector was functioning, running through his presentation in the room, and then standing in front of the audience and delivering his speech. He saw himself forgetting what to say, but recovering quickly when he referred to his prompt card. After imagining this scenario ten times he felt more confident that he would be able to cope and deliver an acceptable presentation. He practised this exercise daily.

Coping imagery can also be useful to prevent negative images raising stress levels, and therefore becoming self-fulfilling prophecies. For example the technique can be used by parents to help children calm their nerves before an exam, or by managers to help their employees to deal with a range of problems.

Motivation imagery

Motivation imagery was developed by Palmer and Neenan (1998) to help de-motivated people gear themselves up for action. It can be used for both personal and work-related problems. The first stage is to imagine not doing what you want to do for the rest of your life, and secondly visualise actually doing what you want to do.

Exercise

Think about an area in your life that you could improve by taking action, which until now you have avoided. This might include moving out of rented accommodation and buying your first house, or applying for a promotion at work.

- Next visualise yourself for the rest of your life not undertaking the change. What effect will it have on you or your friends and family? What regrets would you have if you did nothing?
- Now, imagine yourself doing what you would like to do and think about the short- and long-term benefits that the change would make to your life.
- Finally, consider how you are going to put the change into action.

It is important to visualise the 'inaction' imagery before the 'action' imagery, in order to motivate yourself and help pull you out of a stressful rut.

Case study

Anne was unhappy in the job she had been doing for nearly eight years. She found it no longer stimulated or challenged her. Opportunities often arose for her to apply for a promotion but Anne's anxiety about not being successful in a new post was a blocking emotion, preventing her from moving on. A new job would not only provide Anne with more income, but the challenge and opportunity for personal development she was after. Anne decided to use self-motivation imagery.

Anne first imagined (inaction imagery) herself never changing her job for the rest of her life, believing that she was a failure. She imagined herself becoming very bored in her job and consequently becoming de-motivated thereby under-performing. She saw her peers around her progressing and this made Anne feel even unhappier. Then Anne imagined (action imagery) how she would feel if she were to be promoted. Anne began visualising herself being excited about arriving in the office in the morning; chairing meetings, writing important reports, contributing more to the company's profits; with her increased income she could afford to refit the kitchen; and overall she was happier in herself. Although she might make a few mistakes, it was 'not the end of the world' and she would 'not be a failure'. Now Ann was motivated to apply for another job. She then used coping imagery to help deal with a possible job interview.

Time projection imagery

People often lose their perspective of a stressful situation such as a relationship break-up or losing a job. However, losing sight of the reality or blowing things out of proportion does not allow them to deal with the event in a constructive way. This imagery technique helps to 'de-awfulise' these situations and helps to put them back into perspective (Lazarus, 1984).

Time projection exercise
Below are six steps to follow (Palmer & Strickland, 1996):
    1. Think of the stressful situation or problem.

2. Imagine yourself in three months' time. Will the current situation be as stressful as it is now?

3. Imagine yourself in six months' time. Will you be under the same degree of stress? Can you see yourself getting on with your life?

4. Imagine yourself in a year's time. Will you be under the same degree of stress? Can you see yourself getting on with your life?

5. Imagine yourself in two years' time. Will you be under the same degree of stress? Can you picture yourself doing another job that you enjoy? Can you picture yourself meeting new people? Can you see yourself having fun again?

6. Imagine yourself in five years' time. Will the significance of the current event have decreased? Will it have become less memorable? If you still find it hard to picture a positive future, visualise having the new job or a new relationship, or whatever is appropriate.

Case study

Sarah had recently separated from her long-term boyfriend, Richard. She naturally felt very distressed and upset. She was unable to envisage ever having a relationship again; or believe any other person would want to date her in the future. Sarah used time projection imagery to help herself through this difficult situation.

Sarah started by imagining herself in three months' time; taking that holiday in Prague she wanted to do but Richard was never keen on. She imagined spending more time with her girlfriends again. And by thinking forward to six months' time, Sarah could see herself having moved house to be nearer to her family and friends again. By looking forward to a year's time Sarah could see how she would have joined local clubs and societies and meet new people. By the end of the exercise Sarah was able to believe that in five years' time the significance of splitting up with Richard would not be as great, as she was able to see how her life may move on from where it was. This served to reduce Sarah's stress levels and to help her to come to terms with her separation from Richard.

Relaxation imagery

Imagery can also be used as a relaxation technique. Try the technique below (Palmer & Strickland, 1996).

This method helps to achieve a relaxed state of body and mind. It centres on imagining yourself in your favourite relaxing place such as walking on a beach or sitting in a deck-chair in your garden. To use this technique follow the steps below.

Exercise

1. Find a place where there is as little noise as possible, and you will not be disturbed.

2. Either lie or sit in a comfortable position.

3. Close your eyes and picture your favourite relaxing place.

4. Concentrate on the colours in this place.

5. Concentrate on one particular colour.

6. Concentrate on the sounds in your place. It may be silence.

7. Imagine touching something in your place.

8. Concentrate on the aromas in your place.

9. When you are ready, open your eyes.

If you practise this method regularly, you will be able to achieve a relaxed state quickly and with minimal effort. This technique is also very helpful if you are experiencing sleeping difficulties.

Imaginal exposure

Imagery techniques can also be used to help you overcome a phobia. This is a similar approach to the graded behavioural exposure explained in Chapter 3. It involves imagining yourself in the varying degrees of a feared situation. In many circumstances it is also useful to imagine yourself in the feared situation and habituating at each stage before exposing yourself to the real life fear.

Exercise – Hierarchy of fears

Identify the key events or items about which you are most anxious in relation to your phobia. For each item use a rating (SUD) scale of 0–10, where 0 represents no anxiety, and 10 represents high anxiety or panic.

Next either imagine yourself in each of the events in your list or put yourself in the situation, and stay at each stage until your levels of anxiety reduce and you feel ready to move on to the next item in your hierarchy.

Case study

Helen worked for a law company. She had flown once before with her husband on their honeymoon and had become very anxious as they had experienced a turbulent flight. Since that time, she had avoided travelling by plane. However her company had just asked her to speak at a conference in America. It was a fantastic career opportunity and one she knew she wanted to do. She knew she would not be able to travel by sea and a flight was the only option.

Firstly Helen listed her hierarchy of fears, see the list below.

Rank	Subjective units of distress (SUDs)	Event/item
1	10.0	Take off
2	9.5	Turbulence
3	9	The noise of the engines during take off
4	8.5	Flying at night
5	8	Listening to the safety procedure
6	7.5	Hearing how high they were flying
7	7	Flying in rain
8	6.5	Plane touching down
9	6	Aircraft door being shut
10	5.5	Queuing to enter the plane

Helen decided to start her graded exposure programme using her imagination as this was more appropriate than experiencing the real events. Helen sat at home in a comfortable chair and closed her eyes and began imagining herself standing in the queue waiting to board the plane. After about 10 minutes, her levels of anxiety decreased and she began to feel only a little anxious (score 1). She then imagined sitting on the plane and seeing the aircraft door being shut. Again, after about 10 minutes she felt only a little anxious so she felt ready to imagine the plane landing and having survived the flight. This triggered a great deal of anxiety and took a while longer before Helen felt less anxious (score 3). Finally, she was able to imagine herself on the plane with the rain pounding against the window, and once she felt OK with this event she was able to move onto the next item. However, imagining being told how high the plane was flying took longer for Helen to get used to as it elicited a huge degree of anxiety. Not surprisingly, Helen felt tired after this exercise and decided to stop and return to the programme the next day. The following morning Helen returned to the exercise and started again at her ranking of 7, rain against the window, just to ensure she had conquered this anticipatory fear. Then she continued up the list in the same way she had the day before. By the third day of working on this, Helen felt able to cope with imagining flying at night, through turbulence and hearing the noises of the engines. On the fourth day she was able to tolerate imagining taking off flying into turbulence and rain simultaneously.

Before her trip, Helen also visited her local airport and watched and listened to planes landing and taking off. Each time as her anxiety reduced her confidence increased. She also recorded the sounds of the planes on her tape recorder so she could listen at home. Within a week, Helen felt able to take her trip to the States and speak at the conference.

For further information and self-help techniques to deal with fear of travelling, refer to: Stress-free flying (Bor et al., 2000) or Living with fear (Marks, 1980).

Conclusion

Imagery exercises have been shown to help people deal with predicted crises, overcome phobias, put current situations into perspective, and help us to relax. However, in our experience, most people who are stressed regularly practise catastrophic imagery of events going badly wrong. No wonder they make mountains out of molehills! Negative pictures trigger negative emotions such as anxiety (Lazarus, 1984). This chapter has illustrated how with the application of techniques or methods suggested, you will be able to cope or overcome many anxiety-provoking problems and learn how to relax. Of course, just like any other skill such as driving, daily practice is essential.

Exercise

Now you have finished this chapter, please complete the section below.

What problems do you wish to resolve or manage?

What techniques or strategies do you wish to use to help you deal with the problems noted above?

7
Cognitive techniques and strategies

This chapter will help you to deal with the cognitive responses to stress. You will find the techniques described in this section particularly useful if you have ever found yourself thinking you 'can't stand' a situation any more because 'it's awful'. Or found yourself feeling very angry with a person you think is 'totally stupid'?

If you have experienced thoughts such as these you may have been susceptible to one of the fourteen common thinking errors, which have been identified by psychologists. Researchers have found that when a person becomes stressed they usually have negative thoughts, which in turn prevent them from being able to resolve the situation effectively. By identifying what these thinking errors are stress levels can be reduced. This theory supports the model of stress outlined in Chapter 2, explaining how it is the way we perceive the external event or pressure that largely contributes to the stress (Ellis et al., 1997).

Thinking errors

Below is a list of the 14 common thinking errors. As you read them, ask yourself whether you have ever thought these, or whether one or more of these errors has ever prevented you from successfully resolving a problem.

Labelling
Globally labelling yourself or other people frequently in a degrading way, instead of rating a person's skills or behaviours. For example, 'Because I've failed my driving test, I am totally stupid and a complete failure'. Or 'My assistant has forgotten to order tea and coffee again – this just shows he is incompetent'.

All-or-nothing thinking

Seeing things only in extreme terms with no middle ground. For example, 'If I'm going to buy a new PC, I may as well buy the top of the range' or 'I'm going to leave my job because I don't like my boss'.

Focusing on the negative

Only seeing the negative aspects of an event or situation, whilst ignoring the positive and failing to keep events in perspective. For example, only dwelling on the negative feedback given in a job appraisal, rather than focusing on the positive comments; 'I'm always late and can't reach my deadlines', or ignoring any positive feedback given by teachers at your child's parents' evening; 'My child is failing at school'.

Discounting the positive

Choosing to consider all positive events as unimportant and disregarding them. For example, 'I only won the swimming race because I was lucky' rather than acknowledging that you trained hard. Or 'My manager only gave me a good appraisal because she thinks I'll leave – she doesn't really mean it'.

Magnification

Blowing an event, and the significance of it, out of all proportion. Often involves emphasising the negative, therefore sometimes known as 'awfulising'. For example, 'If I don't deliver that report to my manager on time, it will be absolutely awful' or 'If I don't pay my telephone bill on time it will be the end of the world'.

Minimisation

This is the opposite of magnification and involves playing down the importance of our skills and strengths. For example, 'Getting the job was nothing to be proud of – it was down to luck really' or 'although the starter I cooked for my dinner party was OK, the rest of the meal was diabolical'.

Mind-reading

Making assumptions that people are either reacting or thinking negatively towards us based on little evidence or their behaviour. For example, 'My friend didn't say "hello" to me in the supermarket today, I've obviously upset her' or 'My manager clearly doesn't trust me to manage my department'.

Fortune-telling

Predicting the outcome for events despite the fact there is a lack of evidence to support this. For example, 'I have a huge workload this week. I'm bound to screw up!' or 'What's the point in washing my car as it's bound to rain today'.

Personalisation

Taking the blame for an outcome for which we are not entirely responsible. For example, 'My team didn't get their bonus, I can only blame myself'. Or 'my children have underachieved at school. It's all my fault'.

Blame

This is the opposite of personalisation. This is where you blame others ignoring any personal responsibility your own behaviours or attitudes may have on the outcome. For example, 'My assistant should have known where that letter was on my desk' or 'Why didn't you pay the bills on time?'.

Emotional reasoning

Evaluating a situation purely based on how you feel emotionally. For example, 'I feel so anxious. This proves I'm going to lose my job' or 'I feel like an idiot so I must be one'.

Over-generalisation

Taking one unfortunate event and making sweeping, generalised conclusions about all other events based on this. For example, 'Because I didn't get that job, I'll be turned down for others I apply for' or 'Because I failed my driving test for the first time, I'll fail all subsequent tests'.

'I-can't-stand-it-itis'

By telling ourselves 'I can't stand it' or 'I can't bear it', you lower your tolerance of dealing with difficult or frustrating problems. For example, 'I can't stand my desk being near the main door to the office' or 'I can't bear being on my own in the house in the evening'.

'Demanding-ness'

This occurs when you hold rigid and fixed beliefs often resulting in unrealistic expectations. These are usually expressed as 'shoulds', 'musts', 'got tos', 'have tos' and 'oughts'. For example, 'I must always do all the tasks my manager tells me to do' or 'My children must pass their exams and go to university'.

Exercise – Thinking errors audit

Psychologists, Professor Cooper and Professor Palmer (2000) advocate undertaking a personal audit of thinking errors. Think about a current problem you are stressed about or a previous stress scenario. Note down what your stress-inducing beliefs are. Next, note the thinking errors you recognise in yourself.

Stress-inducing thoughts

_____

_____

_____

_____

Thinking errors   Your example

Labelling

_____

All-or-nothing thinking

_____

Focusing on the negative

_____

Discounting the positive

_____

Magnification

_____

Minimisation

_____

Mind-reading

_____

Fortune-telling

_____

Personalisation

_____

Blame

_____

Emotional reasoning

_____

Over-generalisation

_____

'I-can't-stand-it-itis'

_____

'Demanding-ness'

_____

Once you can identify what your thinking errors are when under stress, you will be in a better position to appraise the problem or pressures more realistically or even avoid the thoughts all together. This process helps to distance you from your thoughts.

'It's all positive thinking!'

Having identified the thinking errors you regularly use you may be wondering what you do now? There are strategies and techniques that can be used to help you break the pattern of these thinking errors (Neenan and Dryden, 2002). Recent research has also shown that using cognitive techniques (such as thinking skills) to modify unhelpful thinking, can help to reduce anxiety, fight stress and depression. It is important to note these thinking skills are not the same as positive thinking. For example, positive thinking would be saying 'It will be alright on the day', whereas a more realistic thought would be 'Things may go wrong on the day. I'll prepare for them before the event'. In other words, thinking skills are about being realistic and keeping events in perspective. Like any skill, they require practice and hard work in order to acquire them.

Thinking skills
Below are eight 'thinking skills' that will help to modify and dispel the thinking errors described earlier.

De-labelling
If you find yourself saying; 'I'm a complete idiot' or 'He's a total failure', do you find this helpful in dealing with the situation? Does this think-

ing motivate or de-motivate you? As you use these phrases do they decrease or increase your stress levels?

Step back and ask how realistic and valid these global labels are? Are they an accurate description? For example, to be a 'complete idiot', you would need to be idiotic at everything you did every single day – and this would be extremely hard, if not impossible, to achieve. It would be more accurate to state, 'Although at the meeting, I acted idiotically, it does not mean I'm a complete idiot'. Likewise, instead of 'As he has failed to reach the deadline, he's a total failure', a more realistic belief could be 'Although he has failed to reach the deadline this does not mean he is a total failure as a manager. He has performed well on other occasions'. And if your partner has locked his car keys in the car, this does not necessarily mean he is totally stupid, merely he has perhaps acted stupidly on this occasion.

It is important you rate the behaviour or the skills deficits and not the person. After all, fallibility is simply part of being human!

Befriend yourself

This is probably one of the most powerful thinking skills to counter unhelpful thoughts. So often we are unfairly critical of ourselves. If you make an important error, think about what you would say if a colleague or friend had made the same error. The chances are you would not be so harsh or critical. So instead of thinking, 'I was hopeless at the job interview', stand back and think about it more realistically, 'Although I could not answer all the questions, in the circumstances, I gave it my best shot. At least it was good practice for my next interview'. In other words, turn your internal critical voice around and do not ignore the positive aspects.

Relative thinking

If you find you are evaluating a situation in extreme terms, such as dreadful versus fantastic, relative thinking is about finding the middle ground. This will help to keep events in perspective. On the whole, people and most situations are too complex to view and categorise in such extreme terms. For example, if you are saying, 'I will never be able to do that task', think about the aspects of the task that you can do. 'I can write the report and submit it on time. Even though it might not be perfect, it will be good enough for my supervisor'.

Look for evidence

Challenge your stress-inducing ideas by looking for evidence, instead of making assumptions. Ask your friends, family or colleagues for feedback about a task you have undertaken such as chairing a meeting, or giving a wedding speech. You can also test assumptions by deploying behavioural interventions, for example, if you believe 'I can't stand waiting for a train', make yourself arrive at the station earlier or wait for the next train. This will provide you with living proof you are able to stand the waiting, even if you do not particularly like it. It is important to avoid mind reading.

Broaden the picture

If things go wrong, we often apportion blame to ourselves (personalisation), or a completely innocent bystander (blame). However, if you do blame yourself or others, it is important that problems are rarely the responsibility of one person.

A useful technique to challenge personalisation or blame is to note down all the individuals or issues involved and then represent these different people and issues graphically on a pie chart. This will allow you to allocate everybody's responsibility for what happened including yourself.

Case study

Situation: Maureen was the manager of a large team. Maureen's department failed to reach their target and she felt totally responsible for the situation (personalisation) (see pie chart below). Maureen then used the 'broaden the picture' technique and realised she was not completely responsible (see pie chart at top of page 61) and there were other factors that had contributed to the team not meeting their target.

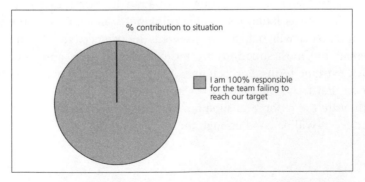

% contribution to situation

I am 100% responsible for the team failing to reach our target

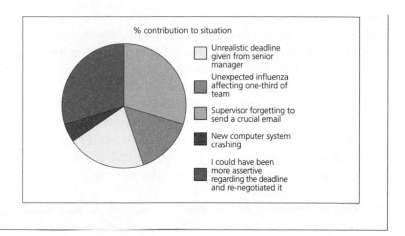

% contribution to situation

- Unrealistic deadline given from senior manager
- Unexpected influenza affecting one-third of team
- Supervisor forgetting to send a crucial email
- New computer system crashing
- I could have been more assertive regarding the deadline and re-negotiated it

Case study

Situation: Robert's teenage son had just failed his exams. Robert completely blamed his son (blame) (see pie chart below). However on reflection once he had broadened the picture, he realised he was not completely to blame (see bottom pie chart), and there were in fact other aspects that had contributed to the situation.

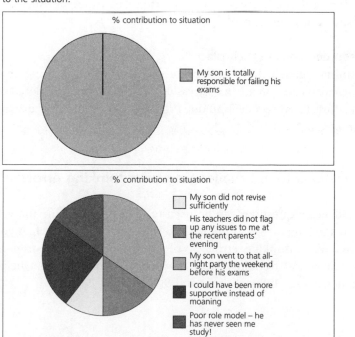

% contribution to situation

- My son is totally responsible for failing his exams

% contribution to situation

- My son did not revise sufficiently
- His teachers did not flag up any issues to me at the recent parents' evening
- My son went to that all-night party the weekend before his exams
- I could have been more supportive instead of moaning
- Poor role model – he has never seen me study!

Demagnification or 'deawfulising'

It is very easy to blow a situation out of all proportion and this will only serve to increase your stress levels. That is not to say events may be difficult to deal with, or unfortunate, but ask yourself, 'Is it really awful?', 'Is it the end of the world?', or 'Is this a hassle or a horror?' By examining a situation and rating it appropriately you can learn to lessen your stress response. 'This is awful! I've missed my train and I'll be late for the appointment' versus 'It's a real hassle that I'm going to be late for the appointment. However, it's not the end of the world. Now I'll concentrate on what I can leave out of the meeting.'

Thinking more 'coolly' or 'flexibly'

This skill can be difficult to master if you are a person who holds inflexible, absolutist and dogmatic beliefs in your head. Yet these negative and demanding beliefs can trigger high levels of stress and are often expressed with emotive language such as, 'My child must go to university'. This not only places more stress on you, it also places pressure on your child. Thinking more 'coolly' will help to reduce the stress, for example, 'I would strongly prefer my child to go to university. However, it's not a disaster if he doesn't.' In other words introduce more flexible and realistic beliefs into your repertoire of thoughts, such as wants, desires and preferences.

Keep emotions in their place

Remind yourself that just because you are feeling a strong emotion, it does not mean you are in a 'stressful' or threatening situation. For example, 'just because I feel anxious it does not mean that driving is life threatening'.

Questions to aid challenging your thinking errors

Challenging questions can be used to help you examine the validity of your thinking errors. Think back to the earlier exercise when you noted down your thinking errors. Write down below your stress-inducing statement and thinking error. Then choose questions that help you to challenge its validity (Palmer and Strickland, 1996).

Is the belief logical?

- Would a scientist agree with my logic?
- Am I thinking logically?
- Am I labelling myself, somebody or something else? Is this a logical thing to do?

Is the belief realistic (empirically correct)?

- Where is the evidence for my belief?
- Would people I know agree with my idea?
- Is the situation so awful or terrible? What is making it feel this way?
- Am I making a big deal of this? Am I blowing it out of proportion?
- If I 'can't stand it', what will really happen?

Is the belief helpful?

- Where is my attitude getting me?
- Is it helping me attain my goals?
- Is my belief helping me to solve my problem?
- Am I placing demands on others or myself? Is this helpful and constructive?
- Am I taking things too personally?

Stress Thought Record

Another helpful technique is to keep a stress thought record. This involves making a note of what stress-inducing thoughts or thinking errors you are experiencing. These can be referred to as Stress Inducing Thinking (SIT). Once you have identified which thoughts are exacerbating your stress you can begin to apply the thinking skills discussed previously, and develop thoughts to alleviate the stress, known as Stress Alleviating Thinking (SAT) (developed by Neenan and Palmer, Centre for Stress Management).

Below is an example of a Stress Thought Record. Complete the blank form for a problem you wish to feel less stressed about.

PROBLEM: *Possible redundancy*

Stress Inducing Thinking (SIT)	Stress Alleviating Thinking (SAT)
Redundancy could impact upon my family and finances	*Worrying won't decrease the likelihood of redundancy – it will probably make it worse if anything. I have lots of skills – if I were made redundant I shouldn't have too much of a problem finding other employment*

This shouldn't happen to me	Why shouldn't it? The reality is that cut-backs may have to be made
The company should look after its staff	The company has everyone to consider – it's not personal to me
They are treating me so badly after all the years I've worked for them	Are they? I'm taking this rather personally. It won't help me! Other ideas When worry occurs at work, tell myself that, 'there's nothing I can do about it right now' Perhaps use 10 minutes worry time in the evening before dinner
	Use problem-solving skills to work on employment situation and revise financial situation. Ask for break in mortgage payments
© Centre for Stress Management, 2002	Update CV and scan papers for jobs.

PROBLEM:

Stress Inducing Thinking (SIT)	Stress Alleviating Thinking (SAT)

© Centre for Stress Management, 2002

Improving performance

If you are concerned with improving your performance in an area of your personal or work life, it is important to note down your own performance interfering thoughts (PITs) and then modify them to performance enhancing thoughts (PETs). This is similar to using the stress thought record. A completed Enhancing Performance form is below.

Enhancing performance

Problem: *Unable to start writing my dissertation*	
Performance Interfering Thinking (PIT)	**Performance Enhancing Thinking (PET)**
I can't start writing until I'm sure of all the facts.	*Strictly speaking, is this true?* *I could start writing the chapter on research first and then return to the earlier chapters*
I must ensure I have all the information I need before I start writing	*Must I?* *Is this realistic?* *Where is it written that I 'must' have all the facts? (Inside my head)* *Even if I did have all the information, how on earth would I use it all?* *I doubt that surfing the internet is really helping me!*
It must be perfect!	*Again, is this realistic?* *Are the examiners looking for 100% perfection?* *Perhaps only I am looking for perfection. If I don't start then that's certainly not perfect!* *Perhaps 'good enough' will do.*
If I fail my doctorate, then this proves I'm a failure	*Is this logical?* *Can failing at one major event prove I'm a failure as a person?* *Anyway, I'm more likely to fail if I do nothing!*
© Centre for Stress Management 2002	

Exercise

Think of a situation that you commonly experience and wish to improve your performance. Note down below in the PIT column, any thoughts, attitudes or thinking errors you have that reduce or interfere with your performance. Then use the questions to aid challenging your thinking errors from the earlier section to help you modify your ideas. Then write down in the PET column your performance enhancing thoughts

Enhancing performance

Problem:	
Performance Interfering Thinking (PIT)	**Performance Enhancing Thinking (PET)**

© Centre for Stress Management 2002

Self esteem versus self-acceptance

Another cognitive response to stress is related to self-esteem. In our clinical and coaching experience we have found that one of the main causes of stress for people of all ages is related to having a strong belief in the concept of self-esteem. People often use external factors to enhance their self-esteem, and the main factors in Western society are (Palmer, 1997b):

- Achievement, e.g. obtaining professional qualifications, passing exams
- Good physical characteristics
- Owning property
- Having a good relationship with people of significant importance e.g. partner, family, manager or colleagues
- Rewarding career or job
- Competent in an area which is personally significant
- Being approved by people of significant importance
- Being a good parent/friend/colleague
- Being a good partner/lover
- Practising a religious faith

On the whole, people tend to esteem themselves more highly when they have or acquire a possession or item of personal significance, such as a prestigious job, qualifications, a healthy physique, an attractive partner and so on. Conversely they 'dis-esteem' themselves when they do not have or lose a possession or item of personal significance. The problem with linking your self-esteem with external aspects or factors is that in life people are likely to lose some of these factors, such as a job or grow old and lose their youthful looks, or not be as skilled at an activity that they believe is important for them to excel at such as parenting skills. According to Palmer (1997b) the over-riding problem with the self-esteem trap is you feel good about yourself when things in life are going well and bad when they are not. So what can you do?

In our experience we have found that a philosophy of self-acceptance can help to reduce stress because it avoids the ups and downs of self-esteem. Self-acceptance is about accepting yourself 'warts and all' and acknowledging one of the key aspects that makes us human is that we are fallible and not perfect (Lazarus, 1977).

For example, instead of thinking, 'If my partner leaves me I'm a complete failure' you could instead think, 'If my partner leaves me it's a huge disappointment but it does not mean I'm a failure'.

By deploying these techniques you can help yourself and others, both in your personal and work life to identify and deal with some of the common cognitive stress responses.

Shame-attacking exercises

Shame-attacking exercises were developed by Dr Albert Ellis (Ellis et al., 1997; Ellis, 2001). They can help people who 'dis-esteem' themselves if they think or act negatively. Shame-attacking refers to acting in a manner which you regard as 'shameful' or embarrassing and challenging the beliefs that are underlying this feeling of being ashamed. For example, if you dis-esteem yourself when you act stupidly you can put yourself in a situation where you may experience the shame of being laughed at. For instance, stand on a street corner by the street name sign and ask passers-by how to find that specific street. This may induce a passer-by to laugh at you or you may mind read that they think you are stupid. You could read out aloud poems on a train. However, it is important to develop a coping statement prior to the shame attacking exercise. For example, you can challenge your unhelpful shame-inducing beliefs by saying to yourself: 'Just because these people are laughing at me or think I'm totally stupid, it doesn't prove that I am stupid. I don't need to feel ashamed. Even if these people may think I'm stupid I can still accept myself. I am not my behaviour!' Incidentally, it is important not to take any risks that could involve upsetting others, losing your job, or breaking the law. Technically speaking, shame-attacking is an interpersonal or behavioural intervention but we include it in this chapter as it is a great exercise to help reinforce the concept of self-acceptance.

Conclusion

For many of the people we have helped over the years to tackle stress, the idea that we can moderate our troublesome emotions by changing our beliefs has been surprising, yet also empowering. For many situations or life events that arise, it becomes apparent that we have more emotional responsibility than we originally would have considered. It has enabled our clients to shed the victim role and decide to deal with difficult situations. In the work place, by challenging PITs and developing PETs, procrastination decreases and performance improves.

Exercise

Now you have finished this chapter, please complete the section below.

What problems do you wish to resolve or manage?

What techniques or strategies do you wish to use to help you deal with the problems noted above?

8

Interpersonal techniques and strategies

This chapter covers techniques to deal with the way we respond inter-personally to stress. It examines how we interact with other people when feeling stressed and looks at methods to modify these and improve our interactions. Many people become very aggressive when feeling stressed, whilst others feel so low they become completely passive. Other people simply find it difficult to talk to or communicate with others. The chapter explains methods to improve assertiveness, make use of your social support network, and enhance your communications skills.

Assertiveness

Being assertive is an important aspect of stress management because it enables you to counter some of the pressures that lead to stress. But it is important to differentiate between assertiveness and aggression. People who are aggressive often think they are being assertive because they are 'standing up for themselves', however, often this is not the case. Aggressive behaviour does not help deal with interpersonal interactions effectively because being aggressive violates the rights of others and causes conflict in relationships both at work and at home. In contrast people who are non-aggressive (passive) have difficulty in standing up for themselves and therefore frequently find they are walked over by others. This tends to lead to resentment.

Assertive behaviour involves being able to ask for what you want, stand up for yourself, provide constructive feedback and complain appropriately. It can be defined as 'behaviour that helps us to communicate clearly and confidently our needs, wants, and feelings to other people without abusing in any way their human rights' (Lindenfield, 1986). As a consequence assertive behaviour is likely to avoid situations such as resentment, misunderstanding and exploitation.

Exercise

Below is a table describing some of the behaviours and the common language used by people who are aggressive, passive and assertive. When you read through, think of a difficult situation you have encountered recently and tick which of these behaviours you displayed.

Aggressive Behaviour

Thumping of fists ❏
Shouting ❏
Pointing finger ❏
Leaning forward ❏
Dominating ❏

Language

You should/ought/must ❏
That's stupid ❏
It's your fault ❏
You've got to be joking ❏

Passive Behaviour

Hand-wringing ❏
Giggling voice ❏
Downcast eyes ❏
Hunched shoulders ❏
Shrugging ❏
Stepping backwards ❏

Language

It doesn't matter ❏
Maybe ❏
Perhaps ❏
Never mind, it's not important ❏
I wonder if I could ❏
Oh forget it ❏

Assertive Behaviour

Behaving in a relaxed and unhostile manner ❏
Smiling when pleased ❏
Behaving in a collaborative way as opposed to a competitive way ❏
Giving and receiving compliments ❏

Language

Use of 'I' statements – 'I think', 'I feel' or 'I want' ❏
'Let's' or 'we could' ❏
Using open questions (those not requiring a 'yes' or 'no' answer) such as 'What do you think?' ❏
(Adapted from Palmer and Strickland, 1996)

By learning to communicate in an assertive way you can express your preferences, feelings and needs in a way that enhances your relationships, and hence improve your interpersonal skills. It allows you to communicate in a direct and honest way, showing you can relate to people as equals and avoid misunderstandings, thus reducing stress.

Learning assertiveness skills

It is possible to change passive or aggressive behaviour and become assertive. But it is not easy to change the way you have behaved for a lifetime and it takes determination, practice and motivation, coupled with a belief in your assertive rights.

There are a number of 'assertiveness rights' that have been identified. These are shown below (taken from Palmer and Strickland, 1996).

- The right to say 'no'
- The right to consider my own needs as important
- The right to make mistakes
- The right to take responsibility for my actions
- The right not to understand
- The right to be me
- The right to set my own priorities
- The right to respect myself
- The right to be assertive without feeling guilty
- The right to express my feelings in an appropriate manner without violating anybody else's rights
- The right not to be assertive when I so choose

Assertion techniques

In this section we include four techniques that can be used to develop your assertiveness skills. The examples illustrate how you can use assertiveness skills to deal with a number of different situations.

Fogging
This involves differentiating between genuine points of criticism that require attention, and manipulative or irrelevant 'put-downs'. It helps to maintain self-respect.

For example:

Your manager: 'You never manage to get to the team meeting on time and this sets a bad example to the others'.

You: 'I've been late twice for our meetings in the past two months. This does not appear to have a bad effect on the team'.

Broken record

Broken record involves stating your views as if you were a 'broken record', repeating what you wish to say and not deviating from the point by irrelevant arguments. This is a useful strategy to use when facing conflict or someone else is putting pressure on you to do a task you do not want to do. It allows you to express your point in a calm manner and ignore provocation.

For example:

Customer: 'Oh, come on let me in, I only need to buy two items'

Shop-owner: 'Unfortunately we shut ten minutes ago and I've already cashed the till.'

Customer: 'Come on. Be reasonable.'

Shop-owner: 'I've closed the shop and till already. I don't serve after 5 o'clock'.

Workable compromise

Assuming your self-respect is not being challenged; this method involves offering a compromise.

For example:

Manager: 'We need to finish this project by tomorrow. Can you stay late this evening to finish it?'

You: 'I am going to the cinema this evening. I could come in earlier tomorrow though and have it finished by lunchtime. Is that OK?'

Negative inquiry

Negative inquiry involves seeking specific and constructive feedback by picking up on someone's negative, often global, feedback.

For example:

Manager: 'You are useless as a supervisor!'

Supervisor: 'Can you tell me in what way I am useless?'

Use of social support

Social support has been found by researchers to be a good buffer against stress. This section considers what social support you use when dealing with your personal and work problems. If you have a work based problem, it is often best to speak to someone who is task-focused, whereas home or personal issues may require someone who will be sympathetic.

Complete the social support questionnaire below to assess your support network.

It can be useful to think about whom you can rely on for support when problems arise. Think who from your support network of family, friends, and colleagues you could talk to if you had a work problem; a family problem; felt stressed; were facing a crisis; or had health problems. This will help you to realise whether your support network is appropriate or not.

Social Support Questionnaire

Social Support: Personal problems

Think of a situation which has caused you a great deal of personal stress. To what extent did each of the following help you with the problem?

1 indicates little support; 5 a great deal of social support

Husband/wife, partner	1	2	3	4	5
Mother	1	2	3	4	5
Father	1	2	3	4	5
Sister	1	2	3	4	5
Brother	1	2	3	4	5
Other relative	1	2	3	4	5
Close friend	1	2	3	4	5
Casual friend	1	2	3	4	5
Work colleague	1	2	3	4	5
Doctor/clergy/therapist	1	2	3	4	5

Plot total score below

Low support		High support
0	10	40

Note: a positive score is 10, when one person is assigned 3 or more on the scale.

(Source: Cooper et al., 1998)

Social Support Questionnaire

Social Support: Work problems

Think of a situation at work which has caused you a great deal of stress. To what extent did each of the following help you with the problem? As before '1' indicates little support, '5' a great deal.

Social support:

Husband/wife, partner	1	2	3	4	5
Mother	1	2	3	4	5
Father	1	2	3	4	5
Sister	1	2	3	4	5
Brother	1	2	3	4	5
Other relative	1	2	3	4	5
Close friend	1	2	3	4	5
Casual friend	1	2	3	4	5
Manager/supervisor	1	2	3	4	5
Colleague	1	2	3	4	5
Subordinate	1	2	3	4	5
Doctor/clergy/therapist	1	2	3	4	5

Plot total score below

Low support		High support
0	10	40

Note: a positive score is 10, when one person is assigned 3 or more on the scale.

(Source: Cooper et al., 1998)

The best social support is that which helps you to identify what the problem is and find a way to resolve it. For instance, family members can sometimes be too subjective and not help you to deal with a situation in a constructive manner. However close friends and family may be able to provide a good listening ear when you just want to unload. So it is important to consider the type of issue you have and who is best suited in your social network to help. You may have found you are very reliant on one or two people for your social support, you may feel you would like to address this issue by joining some local clubs or societies of interest and meeting some new people, or ask yourself whether you could discuss your concerns with other people whom perhaps you currently feel unable to. Are there are other people at work you could confide in?

Are there friends from college or a previous job with whom you have lost touch but could work on re-gaining that friendship?

Communications skills

Improving your communications skills can also help to improve the way you interact with people in stressful situations. Many of the skills outlined in the section on assertiveness skills will also help to improve the way you communicate, for example, using the 'assertive' words and phrases.

Other key tips include:

- Allowing both parties to contribute to the conversation – not having one person dominate.
- Difficult conversations or situations can be avoided if you talk regularly and resolve issues and areas of potential conflict before they become an issue.
- If you are given constructive feedback on the way you communicate, find out if there is a way you can improve this area.
- Avoid 'blame' statements. Use 'I' rather than 'you' when talking about your thoughts and feelings.
- Recognise and respect feelings in yourself, only then will you be able to express them clearly.
- Do not assume or make inaccurate inferences. If in doubt about an issue, ask before jumping to the wrong conclusion. Check and confirm understanding.
- Accept responsibility for your actions and behaviours.
- Do not discuss important issues if there is insufficient time to deal with them. Negotiate an alternative time for a discussion.
- Think about what your body language is also saying – it will be saying more about your thoughts and feelings than the words coming out of your mouth.
- Be yourself.

Conclusion

Interpersonal problems at work or home can cause high levels of stress. It is unrealistic to think that we will not encounter interpersonal difficulties at some time in our life. This chapter provided a number of important techniques and strategies to help you deal with the majority of interpersonal problems that may arise. However, regular coping imagery rehearsal, the use of performance enhancing thoughts (PETs), and relaxation techniques may also enhance the application of interpersonal skills.

Exercise

Now you have finished this chapter, please complete the section below.

What problems do you wish to resolve or manage?

What techniques or strategies do you wish to use to help you deal with the problems noted above?

9

Drug-related and biological techniques or strategies

In this chapter we focus on drug-related and biological strategies to deal with stress. Interventions include exercise, nutrition and stopping smoking.

Exercise

In order to see whether this chapter is of relevance to you, complete the questionnaire below. This will help you to assess whether you need to focus on this area of your life.

Healthy living questionnaire

For each of the questions below, focus on the answer that most closely relates to you. The key is:

1 = Never

2 = Rarely

3 = Periodically

4 = Regularly

5 = Very often

Exercise scale

1 Do you do any physical exercise, such as walking, cycling or jogging?

2 Do you take part in any sports activities that involve exerting yourself physically?

3 Do you feel exhausted after physically exerting yourself a little?

4 How often is exercise part of your daily routine?

Nutrition scale

5 How often do you drink more than five cups of tea a day?

6 How often do you drink more than five cups of coffee a day?

7 How often do you eat three meals a day?

8 How often do you eat between meals?

9 How often do you eat fruit and vegetables?

---

10 How often do you eat foods high in saturated fats?

11 How often do you binge-drink alcohol?

Miscellaneous scale

12 Are you under – or over-weight? Yes/No

13 Do you drink more than the recommended weekly guidelines of alcohol (14 units for women and 21 units for men)? Yes/No

14 Do you smoke? Yes/No

Below are the desirable answers:

1   4 or 5
2   4 or 5
3   1 or 2 (consider checking with GP if you have any other result)
4   4 or 5
5   1 or 2
6   1 or 2
7   4 or 5
8   1 or 2
9   4 or 5
10 1 or 2
11 1 or 2
12 No
13 No
14 Preferably no (if yes, rarely!)

(Adapted from: Cooper and Palmer, 2000)

Depending upon how you scored on this questionnaire, you may wish to increase or decrease certain behaviours or activities.

Alcohol

Alcohol depresses the central nervous system. This means, depending on the amount consumed, the short-term effects can include relaxation, reduced motor co-ordination and cognitive ability, mild euphoria, slurred speech and disturbed sleep. In the worst cases it can lead to nausea, vomiting, coma or even death. However, the long-term effects are even more serious and include liver disease, hypertension, heart disease, impaired functioning of the brain, cirrhosis and intestinal bleeding. Some of these disorders can lead to death. Research has shown that the consumption of alcohol in moderation is fine (within the guidelines for the recommended number of units). In fact a couple of units of wine per day, can actually be beneficial because alcohol makes the blood less sticky thus reducing your likelihood of suffering from blood clots or strokes.

The generally accepted maximum recommended consumption of alcohol is 21 units a week for adult males and 14 units a week for adult females. One unit is a glass of wine or half a pint of beer. If you wish to reduce your alcohol intake it can help to keep a dinking diary to monitor your intake. Another useful tip is to purchase non-alcoholic alternatives and drink these when you would normally have alcohol. For example, have a glass of grape juice rather than a glass of wine.

Below is a drinking diary you could use to monitor your consumption (Palmer and Dryden, 1995).

Drinking diary

Date	Beverage	When/where/with whom	Units	Total

Weekly total =

Units (a rough guide)

Wine (11% alcohol content)	standard glass = 1 unit
Ordinary strength beer, lager, cider	half pint = 1 unit; 1 pint = 2 units
Strong beer, lager, cider	half pint = 2 units; 1 pint = 4 units
Sherry	standard small measure = 1 unit
Spirits	standard English measure = 1 unit

Blood Pressure

The average young adult has a blood pressure of 120/80 where the first figure is the 'systolic' blood pressure during each heart beat (contraction of the heart) and the last figure is the 'diastolic' blood pressure as the heart relaxes between the beats (Palmer and Dryden, 1995). The diameter of vessels and the amount of blood being pumped around the system determines the blood pressure. If blood pressure is high for a prolonged period serious health consequences can occur such as strokes, heart attack, renal and arterial diseases.

Hypertension is a chronic disorder when the blood pressure has remained elevated within the arterial blood system for a long period of time. If it has been caused by a specific physical condition such as renal failure, it is known as secondary hypertension. This requires medical attention.

A number of lifestyle behaviours can lead to high blood pressure or hypertension:

- Stress
- Obesity
- Poor nutrition
- Insufficient exercise
- Excessive alcohol consumption
- Type A behaviour P18
- Angry personality
- Genetic predisposition

Essential hypertension is when the cause of the raised blood pressure is unknown. Medication may help and also a number of lifestyle changes. It is important to discuss with your medical advisor possible strategies for reducing blood pressure, see below.

Reducing high blood pressure checklist

- Take up active sports or exercise programme. Join a gym, start fast walking, swimming or jogging
- If overweight, commence a weight reduction and maintenance programme
- Stop smoking
- Ensure alcohol intake is within current guidelines i.e. 14 units a week for females; 21 units a week for males
- Reduce stress in your life. Use relaxation techniques, meditation, breathing exercises or yoga; apply thinking skills to help you keep events in perspective and control anger or frustration; reduce Type A behaviour

Caffeine

In comparison to alcohol, caffeine is a stimulant to the central nervous system. Its consumption can lead to feelings of anxiety, insomnia, increased nervousness and alertness, palpitations, insomnia and restlessness. People with a high intake of caffeine generally benefit from reducing the amount of caffeine they consume. However, it is recommended the reduction is gradual because sudden cessation can cause nausea, headaches and craving for the first 48 hours.

On average the daily intake of caffeine in the UK is about 444 mg (Griffiths and Woodson, 1988). If you would like to reduce your caffeine content it will help to monitor your intake using the table below as a guide. The table illustrates the average caffeine content of various drinks and chocolate (Parrott, 1991: 210).

Dietary source	Average caffeine concentration in 5 oz cup (mg)
Real coffee	100
Instant coffee	70
Tea	40
Cola drink	20
Small chocolate bar	20
Chocolate drink	10
Decaffeinated coffee	3

Although some products can be artificially decaffeinated, Rooibosch tea is naturally low in tannin, caffeine free and high in antioxidants. The latter fight free radicals that can cause damage to cells.

Some research has suggested that moderate tea drinking (between 2 to 5 cups daily) or the consumption of dark chocolate, may reduce the risk of strokes.

Smoking

Smoking is a tremendous stress on the body in every way. Apart from the damage caused by the nicotine and tar found in cigarettes, cigarette smoke consists of about 2,000 chemicals. The toxic metals found in the smoke can interfere with your body's balance of vital minerals such as zinc, iron and copper.

Giving up smoking is extremely stressful for many people. Many people procrastinate by making up excuses about why they cannot give up – 'I'll be impossible to work with,' or 'I'll put on weight'. However, if you want to give up smoking, you need to consider seriously your reasons for stopping. Attempt the exercise below.

Exercise

Write a list of what the immediate advantages are if you were to stop smoking. For example, feeling healthier, saving money, breathing more easily, having fresher breath, tasting food more.

| |
| |
| |
| |
| |

Next consider the future advantages. For example, having fewer chest infections, losing your smoker's cough, experiencing less smoking-related illnesses, reducing the wrinkles on your face, improving the health of the other people in your household.

| |
| |
| |

Now identify the situations that you associate with smoking, such as first thing in the morning, or in the pub. Think of alternatives or ways to avoid those situations. For example, if you have a cigarette with you first cup of coffee, find something else to do such as reading a newspaper or watering the plants.

| |
| |
| |

Once you have completed the exercise above, you will be in a better position to stop smoking because you have considered the reasons for giving up seriously. You may also find that using some of the thinking skills identified in Chapter 7 will help you to address any thinking errors. For example, 'I must have a cigarette' can be replaced by 'I really want a cigarette but I can stand not having one'.

Here are some tips that may help you to stop smoking:

- When you finally decide it is time to stop, pick a 'stop day', preferably a day when you are under as little pressure as possible and begin to reduce the number of cigarettes you have two weeks beforehand.
- Clear your house of all cigarettes, ashtrays and lighters the day before your 'stop day'.
- Start your 'stop day' differently, for example take a short walk.
- Change your routine to avoid situations when a cigarette may seem appealing. Refer to the situations you listed in the exercise.
- At the end of the first day, refer back to the immediate and future benefits for ceasing smoking. Reward yourself, but not with a cigarette!
- Many people do experience mood swings and a cough as their lungs clear. So be prepared for these, and ensure people around you understand too.
- Use nicotine patches or nicotine chewing gum as they can help. However, be aware that these too can become addictive and long-term use should be avoided.
- You may gain weight due to a decrease in your metabolic rate and increased food intake. To prevent this, snack on fruit or other low-calorie foods. Consider undertaking a light physical exercise regime.
- Keep referring back to your list of benefits from the exercise.

Physical Exercise

Exercise can improve your physical and mental health, your self-image and self-esteem, as well as help to manage anger, weight control and stress levels. In our recent study (Palmer, 2000) we found that some participants who undertook regular exercise experienced less occupational stress.

Below are some exercise tips, but please bear in mind if you are over 35 years old, or have any of the following, you should contact your medical practitioner before embarking on a vigorous exercise schedule.

- Pregnant
- Overweight
- Convalescing
- Suffer from asthma
- Have a family history of heart disease
- Have high blood pressure
- Suffer from diabetes
- Experience chest pains

Exercise tips

- It is important to set yourself a gradual programme of exercise. This will be more manageable and you are therefore more likely to meet your goals. If at any time you feel light-headed, dizzy, nauseous, or in pain, stop exercise immediately.
- Warm yourself up before you start exercise by doing gentle stretches and bends. On completing your exercise have a cool down period. Perhaps walk slowly for a couple of minutes.
- Choose sports facilities that are convenient to get to from home or work. And choose exercise that is not wholly dependent on the weather.
- Incorporate exercise into your daily routine. Walk part of your journey, instead of taking transport the whole way.
- To avoid boredom when using exercise equipment, watch television or listen to music.
- Try and put a minimum of twenty minutes aside three times per week.
- Avoid undertaking strenuous exercise within two hours of eating a meal.
- It is easy to feel like giving up your routine if you miss doing it for a couple of weeks owing to home or work commitments or other pressures. If you find yourself in this situation, use the thinking skills discussed in the chapter on cognitive strategies. For example, 'Just because I did not do my exercise this week, it does not mean that I have blown the whole programme (challenging all and nothing thinking).
- Exercise should be pleasurable. Do not set targets that are too difficult to meet. Exercising with other people can be more fun and act as a motivator.

It is worth noting that when a person is under stress cortisol is released into the body. If the person remains stressed over a long period of time the cortisol will have a detrimental effect on the person's immune system, thus increasing their chances of becoming ill (Leonard, and Miller, 1995). Over exercise can also lead to increased cortisol levels and should be avoided. Although athletes may be very fit, they may not be healthy!

Nutrition

As a nation we are becoming more obsessed with our nutrition and weight. Everyday conflicting articles are published on this topic. In this section we will attempt to maintain a balanced view. A poor diet (lacking in essential vitamins and minerals and a high amount of saturated fats) can lead to a variety of illnesses, including coronary heart disease, obesity and digestive problems. People who are feeling unhealthy are also less likely to cope with stress. However, it is important not to allow constant concern about what you eat becoming a stress in itself.

Saturated fats
Saturated fats increase the risk of heart disease because the fat leaves deposits (known as bad blood cholesterol or low-density lipoproteins, LDL) that adhere to the arterial walls that narrow, and eventually may block the arteries. Gradually this may cause an increase in blood pressure and may result in a heart attack. Saturated fats include cheese, milk, lard, butter, and red-meat fat.

Mono-saturated fats
Some fats are not potentially dangerous. Mono-saturated fats do not increase blood cholesterol levels because they do not cause the low density lipo-proteins to be deposited. The main source of these type of fats can be found in avocado pears and olive oil. Research has shown that olive oil may be one of the key contributing factors to the low rate of heart disease found in Mediterranean countries. However, other dietary factors may also be important.

Polyunsaturated fats
Polyunsaturated fats help to reduce blood cholesterol levels and prevent the formation of blood clots. They are found in oily fish such as mack-

erel, sardines or pilchards and various types of vegetable oils such as sunflower, soya or corn oils.

Plant Sterols

Plant sterols are clinically proven to lower your blood cholesterol levels (LDL) by reducing the amount of cholesterol entering the bloodstream from the gut. They work by mixing with the cholesterol in the gut and competing with, thus preventing, the cholesterol being absorbed into the bloodstream. Therefore less cholesterol actually enters the bloodstream, so blood cholesterol levels fall.

Plant sterols are natural substances and can be found in foods such as beans, vegetables, fruit, nuts, and vegetable oils. They do not taste or smell and therefore have no affect on the flavour of the food. They can also be found in some margarine spreads.

Foods

Below is a list of foods to cut down on:

- Full fat cheeses
- Fried food
- Meat products such as pate, burgers and sausages
- White bread
- Biscuits
- Sweetened cereals
- Whole milk
- Cream and yoghurts
- Mayonnaise
- Products with high salt content
- Products with high sugar content

Below is a list of preferred foods:

- Fruit (fresh or in natural juice)
- Low fat cheese
- Grilled, poached or steamed food
- Poultry, fish or lean meat
- Food high in fibre, such as brown rice or bread, beans, pasta and oats. These aid digestion.
- Semi-skimmed or skimmed milk

Weight control

How many diets have you been on? Did they work? For how long did you maintain your desired weight?

Surprisingly diets alone do not work as the majority of people are unable to maintain their desired weight for any length of time. Body weight is increased when the energy taken into the body exceeds that used. Therefore to lose weight, you need to reduce the amount of calorific input into the body and expend more energy by doing more exercise. By maintaining this balance, the desired weight can be achieved. And therein lies the problem. Although this sounds simple, it is deceptively difficult and often requires hard work and perseverance.

There are a number of simple changes that can be made to your lifestyle that can aid the control of weight:

• Avoid snacking between meals
• Cut out foods high in fats and sugars
• Incorporate exercise into your daily routine
• Start exercising regularly

In extreme cases people can become obese. This is a serious threat to health as it can lead to a number of disorders including high blood pressure, heart disease, strokes, diabetes and bronchitis. So controlling your weight is another way to improve your health. The problem comes when people are under stress because many people eat for comfort. It is therefore important to deal with the problem directly and realise that you are comfort eating, to reduce your levels of stress. If you find you do comfort eat when stressed, make sure you do not have un-healthy food in the house.

If you want to lose weight, complete the form below. It will help you to assess the situation, examine what possible changes you may need to make to your lifestyle, and help to focus on the advantages of losing weight.

Weight reduction and control form

For breakfast I usually eat

_____

For lunch I usually eat

_____

For dinner I usually eat

_____

In between meals I usually eat

_____

Circle answers that apply to you:

I regularly eat crisps/biscuits/sweets/pastries/pies/fried food

I regularly eat fibre-rich food such as pasta/wholemeal bread/jacket potatoes/high-fibre cereals

I, or members of my family, have suffered from stroke/diabetes/heart disease/high blood pressure

My weekly consumption of alcohol is _____ units

My sugar intake is low/medium/high

My lifestyle is sedentary/active/very active

Comments and possible changes:

_____

_____

_____

I wish to lose weight because:

_____

_____

_____

(© Palmer, 1988)

Conclusion

The topics raised in this chapter relate directly to health. Interestingly, smoking, comfort eating and alcohol are often used as stress management techniques by many people (Palmer, 2000). Although one or two units a day of alcohol may have some health benefits, an excess of alcohol, poor diet, lack of regular exercise and smoking are not to be recommended. This chapter has provided health choices that are seriously worth acting on.

Exercise

Now you have finished this chapter, please complete the section below.

What problems do you wish to resolve or manage?

What techniques or strategies do you wish to use to help you deal with the problems noted above?

10

Developing your own modality profiles to reduce, manage or eliminate stress

It is possible to use a number of the techniques and strategies explained throughout the last seven chapters to deal with stress-related problems. By noting down your key stress-related problems from each of the seven BASIC I.D. modalities, you can develop your own modality profile which includes possible techniques and interventions to fight stress.

Below are three case studies to demonstrate how modality profiles are developed. They focus on the seven BASIC I.D. modalities covered in chapters 3 to 9:

Behaviour
Affect/emotion
Sensory
Imagery
Cognitive/thoughts/ideas
Interpersonal
Drug-related/biology

Case study

Michael has been asked to give a presentation at the next team meeting. Michael finds giving presentations very stressful and avoids them as far as possible. However, on this occasion it is important he presents, as it will impact on whether or not he is promoted. Below is an example of how he used the various techniques and strategies to deal with his stress.

Modality	Problem	Proposed technique
Behaviour	Procrastination: avoids writing the presentation by doing other tasks such as tidying up files	Uses time management techniques; challenges unhelpful belief about being a failure
Affect/emotional	Feels increased anxiety	Uses feeling identification to ascertain helpful (concern) versus unhelpful (anxiety) emotions
Sensory	Feels sick before giving presentation	Uses relaxation techniques before and during presentation
Imagery	Can only see himself delivering a poor presentation	Uses coping imagery
Cognitive/thoughts/ideas	I must give an excellent presentation (Demandingness) otherwise I will never get promoted (all or nothing) and I will be a failure (label)	Disputes unhelpful beliefs by identifying thinking errors and employing appropriate thinking skills, including self-acceptance training. Complete an Enhancing Performance Form
Interpersonal	Has poor communication skills	Practises and develops communications skills
Drugs/biological	Experiences palpitations and drinks excessive coffee as a way to relax himself	Reduces caffeine intake. Will alternate drinks with decaffeinated coffee

Case study

Sarah has recently become a mother. She is finding adapting to being at home with a baby difficult and is finding herself becoming increasingly angry with herself, her husband and the child. She decides she would like to deal with it because she realises it is not good for her health.

Modality	Problem	Proposed technique
Behaviour	Trying to do too many tasks at once and always rushing (Type A behaviours)	Slow down, focus on one thing at a time
	Eating excessive chocolate	Use stimulus control techniques by removing any chocolate from the house. Have fruit substitutes
Affect/emotional	Feeling over-emotional (angry or tearful) about 'simple' every day events	Use the 'empty chair technique' to practise dealing with situations prior to them occurring

Sensory	Body aching and feeling tense	Have a massage once a week; try self-massage
Imagery	Picture myself as being a bad mother	Use time projection imagery to help see myself with a happy child in the future
Cognitive/thoughts/ideas	I must be a perfect mother (demanding-ness) otherwise I'm a total failure (label), a bad mother (label)	Dispute unhelpful beliefs by identifying thinking errors and employing thinking skills to challenge ideas. Learn self-acceptance
Interpersonal	Has no other new mothers to talk to	Analyse my social support network by doing social support questionnaire. I now realise I am solely reliant on my husband. I'll join some post-natal classes
Drugs/biological	Is not losing the weight gained during pregnancy	Start a gentle exercise regime and improve my diet (and eat more fruit and less chocolate)

Case study

Jayne had tried on three occasions to stop smoking. The first two times she started smoking again only after a couple of weeks. On her last attempt, she was progressing well until she hit a crisis at work. As soon as the pressure was on, she just 'had to have a smoke'. She was determined to give up this time. However, more preparation had to be done to help her deal with the possible causes of the lapse.

Modality	Problem	Proposed technique
Behaviour	Smokes at meal times	Use stimulus control techniques by removing cigarettes, ash tray and lighters from the house. Select a Stop Smoking Day. Cut down smoking to 10 per day for one week prior to the Stop Day.
	Increases smoking when under stress	Learn a range of strategies to manage my stress
Affect/emotional	More easily irritated and quick to feel angry when not smoking	Learn to count to five and breathe slowly when in stressful situations
Sensory	Unpleasant feelings of tension when not smoking	Remember, with time this will pass. Start practising relaxation training before the stop day to help me cope with the tension when it occurs

Imagery	Can picture parents who both smoked	When this picture comes to mind, imagine my parents not smoking
	Picture of father dying in hospital of lung cancer	When I think of smoking again, remind myself of my father dying in hospital
Cognitive/thoughts/ideas	I must have a cigarette when I want one (demandingness)	Dispute unhelpful beliefs: Why must I have a cigarette? Just because I want one doesn't mean I must have one!
	I can't stand unpleasant feelings and tension	This is not true, I don't like it but I'm living proof I can stand these feelings
	I can't stand not smoking	I stood not smoking for 4 weeks the last time. Perhaps I can do better next time?
	If I have one cigarette, then I've blown it. What's the point! (All or nothing thinking)	Just because I have one cigarette, it doesn't mean I've blown it. I don't have to give in
Interpersonal	Smokes in social situations	For the first 6 weeks avoid social situations with friends/colleagues who are smokers
		In role play at home, practise being assertive and saying, 'No, thank you. I don't smoke'. Only when I'm adequately prepared, enter social situations
Drugs/biological	Smokes 40 cigarettes a day	Stop smoking programme. Remind myself of the damage it is doing to my body
	Smoker's cough	Check this out with GP in case of undiagnosed problems
	Lack of exercise	If I stop smoking, it may be a good idea to increase daily exercise as I do not wish to put on additional weight. I can walk up the stairs at work instead of using the elevator. Take a 30 minute walk during my lunch break

These three case studies demonstrate how the techniques and strategies explained in this book can be used in conjunction with one another to deal with a variety of situations that people may perceive as stressful.

Having considered the seven different stress responses and the techniques and strategies to deal with them, we will now look at identifying and dealing with stress at different times in your life. We all experience stress at some point and by knowing what the signs are and deploying the various interventions you can become your own stress management coach, or help others to do the same, as you go through all stages of your life.

Exercise

At the end of the last seven chapters you were asked to complete a simple exercise:

What problems do you wish to resolve or manage?

What techniques or strategies do you wish to use to help you deal with the problems noted above?

Now, look back at your answers to those questions. (If you did not complete them earlier, skim read each chapter and answer the questions.) Complete the Modality Profile Form below.

Modality	Problem	Proposed Technique
Behaviour		
Affect/emotional		
Sensory		

Imagery		
Cognitive, thoughts, ideas		
Interpersonal		
Drugs/biological		

11

Stress in children

Stress in children is on the increase. As is the case with adults, pressure can help a child to perform better at challenges he or she faces, remain more alert and cope better next time the child is in a challenging situation.

So what are the causes? School problems play a large part. Throughout history changing schools has always been stressful for children. But currently as expectations are higher, the children are assessed and tested from a younger age. Not only can the increase in tests or exams contribute to stress levels, the performance in these is important when compared against other children in the class. Bullying is another major cause of stress in children and many schools have attempted to tackle this problem. There is raised awareness of the way a child who is being bullied may behave. The increased awareness surrounding bullying has been positively impacted by the legal requirement for schools in England and Wales now to have an anti-bullying strategy. One of the problems with bullying is that children older than six are less likely to tell parents openly if they are being bullied and keep it a secret. This can be due to anxiety about the possibility of this leading to more bullying.

It has been suggested that with an increase in the number of full-time working parents, children are actually spending less time with their mothers and fathers. According to the psychoanalyst Bowlby (1969), the relationship between infant and caretaker (often the mother or father), is crucial for normal development. If this relationship is disrupted it can lead to the infant displaying protest manifesting itself in characteristics of grief and mourning. This can lead to the child not developing an attachment to its parents, meaning the child could display symptoms of stress.

A child living in a family with problems such as the parents arguing or fighting, or going through a separation, can also cause stress for a child. Children as young as two or three are sensitive to the tensions within their family. And similarly, the death of a family member or pet, as well as the birth of a sibling, can be stressful.

So how can you tell if your child is stressed? Children will show stress in many of the ways discussed earlier in the book. They too will probably display symptoms in all seven response modalities. The problem with children is they may be less able to explain or express themselves so as a parent you need to be aware of other signs to spot. Below are some key symptoms to look out for.

Behavioural signs

- reduced performance at school
- grinding of teeth (especially at night)
- increased crying
- appearing unable to cope with every day life (for example, suddenly finding school difficult to deal with)
- reverting to bed-wetting or thumb-sucking
- increase in clinginess
- not wanting to go to school or truancy

Emotional signs

- tearfulness
- extreme tiredness
- sadness or depression
- swings in mood
- increased irritability
- daydreaming

Sensory signs

These are often harder to spot in children because the signs often require a certain amount of maturity in order for someone to explain the symptoms or be able to identify them. However, symptoms may include:

- complaints of sickness but no actual sickness
- complaints of headaches without any other obvious symptoms
- increased tiredness

Imagery signs

- child complaining of 'nasty' dreams or explaining them in detail
- child continually describing the same picture or image
- child drawing disturbing pictures

Cognitive signs

As with the sensory signs, cognitive responses to stress are often difficult to detect in a child because they may not have the language ability or maturity to express or understand their thoughts in the same way as adults. However signs may be:

- are they blaming themselves more?
- are they blowing little incidents out of proportion?
- is there an inability to concentrate for very long?

Interpersonal signs

- lack of interest in friends
- lack of interest in school activities
- lack of interest in hobbies
- increased sulking behaviour
- reduction in eye contact
- withdrawing into themselves and their own world

Drug-related/biological signs

As with adults, too much stress can have adverse effects on a child's immune system. Therefore signs may include:

- increase in stomach upsets or colds
- limb or joint pains
- more accident prone
- diarrhoea or constipation
- rapid loss or gain of weight

How to deal with child stress

Some children will be able to cope better with challenging situations than others, in the same way adults will. Like adults, a child who has a supportive family and group of friends, is likely to find it easier to deal with difficult situations. Parents can help by providing an informal atmosphere in which the child can talk openly about issues. Or allow your child to talk informally with their friends outside of school. This will encourage them to talk and think through issues. If you are particularly concerned speak to other parents or the school.

Sometimes, parents can be the ones placing unnecessary pressure on their children. Ask yourself are you expecting too much from your child? Are you transferring your un-fulfilled ambitions onto your child? For example, if you did not achieve academic qualifications and now wish you had, are you putting pressure on your child to do so? It is important to be realistic about what your child is able to achieve both academically and socially. When it comes to studying, it is important to encourage your child so they understand the importance of their school work, but it is often better for them to study little and often than engage in long stints. Help them to develop effective and healthy study habits if necessary.

Talking to children about what and why major impending changes are taking place, will help them to deal with the situation when it arises. For example, a child who is shortly to become a brother or sister for the first time is likely to adapt more quickly if they have an understanding about what is happening. An effective technique to talk to very young children is to use story-telling, because they may not be old enough to understand the explanation of what is happening otherwise. It is important however not to tell the child how it will feel.

Many children faced with the separation or divorce of their parents, or the death of a family member, express feelings and thoughts of self-blame (see Personalisation, page 56). For example, 'Mum and Dad are splitting up because of me' or 'Our cat died because of me'. In this situation, even though the parent will be going through a difficult time, it is important to challenge these thoughts and reassure the child the situation that has occurred is not their fault.

If you think your child is stressed in a way you feel unable to deal with or manage, seek help. Your medical practitioner or numerous associations, such as ones dedicated to bullying in schools, will be able to advise you further.

Flying with children

In recent years family package holidays have been an increasingly attractive and feasible option for people with children. Airlines are generally more amenable and the holidays themselves more affordable. However, flying with children can be stressful.

Below are some tips that can help to reduce the stress of flying with children:

- If you are flying with more than one child, allow them to share sitting by the window if appropriate and necessary. Explain this to them in advance to avoid arguing!
- If a child is wishing to go to the toilet more frequently, be supportive as this may indicate excitement or anxiety, or a combination of both!
- If you are travelling with more than one adult, decide in advance who will have responsibility for which child (if you are travelling with two or more children).
- If the child is old enough, involve your children in the packing before the trip. They can even be responsible for packing their own small bag or rucksack.
- If the child is travelling for the first time, prepare them practically and emotionally before the trip. Explain what will happen both once at the airport and on the plane.
- It might also be worth telling them they may experience an odd sensation in their ears and showing them how they can deal with it (swallow, suck sweets, or pinch their nose and blow lightly). If you are travelling with a baby the two methods they have to relieve the discomfort is to cry or swallow, so giving your baby a drink on take-off and landing may be a good idea.
- To avoid boredom ensure the child takes books, toys or music on the plane so they can entertain themselves. If necessary make sure you take enough food and drink also.
- Ensure you also carry medicine to deal with motion sickness. This can include medication, wrist-bands, or ginger tablets (all available from a chemist or health food shop).

12

Studying and procrastination

As mentioned in Chapter 11, many more children are now taking exams. Similarly, there is an increase in the number of teenagers taking qualifications and going onto university. Indeed, more teenagers are taking their driving tests as soon as they are able to do so. Many more adults are also studying, either full-time or part-time whilst also working. Studying and taking exams can be stressful for people of all ages.

When revising or taking an exam, a certain amount of pressure can be good; it can motivate you to revise or perform well in the exam. However, too much pressure can lead to stress which can be detrimental, leading to reduced performance, and at worst a person can become too ill to take the exam.

So what are the causes of study stress? There are many. Research has shown that some people may be more genetically disposed to become highly stressed because they have lower levels of serotonin: a major neurotransmitter (chemical messenger at the end of a nerve) which has a calming effect on behaviour and feelings. When these people are under pressure they are more likely to become anxious and depressed. Some anti-depressants work by modifying the uptake of serotonin. However, this is not to suggest that anyone who experiences study stress should be on medication! There are a number of other ways to manage and reduce the levels of stress experiences.

People who are rigid perfectionists are likely to put themselves under extreme pressure when studying (as well as in the working environment). A perfectionist may use a number of thinking errors that increase their stress levels. For example, the person may be thinking 'I must pass this exam (*demandingness*), otherwise I'm a complete failure' (*labelling*). If the student does not live up to his or her expectations or believes he or she may fail, then the likelihood is that they will cope less well with the current and the following exams. Many of the techniques shown in the chapter on cognitive interventions (Chapter 7) will help in these situations. A more flexible and realistic belief for a person with perfectionist thinking would be to think, 'I really want to pass this exam, but if I fail I can accept myself. It does not mean I'm a total failure, merely someone who did not pass one exam.'

Procrastination

One of the most unhelpful behaviours often displayed by someone feeling stressed about an impending exam is procrastination. People in the work-place can also display this if they are under pressure to finish an important task.

Think back to the last time you had a deadline to meet, or had an exam to revise for. Did you do any of the following activities?

- play computer games
- tidy desk, delete unwanted emails
- clean car
- write a long 'to do' list and commence work on the unimportant items first
- drinks many cups of tea or coffee
- email, ring, talk or whinge to friends or colleagues
- smoke more
- comfort eat
- tell people you work best at the eleventh hour!

As mentioned in Chapter 3, the problem with procrastinating is that it can increase the levels of stress if you want to do well in the exam you are meant to be revising for. By spending time doing any of the unimportant tasks on the list above, you will experience a temporary drop in your stress levels because you are not focusing on or thinking about the task in hand. However, as soon as you stop engaging in the unnecessary task your stress levels will once again soar as you realise you have wasted yet more valuable revision or writing time.

With young people, other causes of study stress can be parental or school pressure with the student believing:

'I must do well otherwise I'll let my family down'.

Challenging these unhelpful beliefs will benefit the person in this situation, for example teach them to think 'Although it is strongly preferable to do well, if I don't, it doesn't mean I've let my family down. This does not make me a failure.'

The responses displayed by a person feeling stressed about studying could manifest themselves in any of the seven BASIC I.D. modalities discussed in the earlier chapters. If you, or someone you know, is feeling stressed about studying, read the seven chapters on the various techniques and strategies and apply those which are most helpful to the individual dependent on how you or they are responding. However, here are some essential tips on how to deal with study stress.

Study stress tips

- Use relaxation techniques. This will help to calm you, especially the night before an exam as it will help to clear your mind of any negative thoughts you may have been thinking.
- Consider the food and drink you consume. Do not drink too much alcohol or coffee the night before. If you eat too late you will go to bed with a full stomach and this may affect your sleep pattern as your body will be digesting your food.
- Devise a revision timetable or plan – but be realistic about what you can achieve in a given time period. Do not spend too long developing the timetable otherwise you may be procrastinating. Reward yourself as you work through your plan.
- If you hold strong perfectionist beliefs, strongly challenge them. Use the thinking skills learnt in the earlier chapter. Use the Enhancing Performance form (Chapter 7).
- If you find you are unable to concentrate in your room because of interruptions from family members or other students, take yourself off to a library. At least there you will find peace and quiet!
- Exercise regularly but moderately.
- Improve the way you manage your time.

Better time management is easy to learn. Here are some ways to improve the way you manage your time:

- Make a list of what you need to achieve before the exam. Refer to the list as you revise and tick items off as you achieve them.
- Divide your work into smaller chunks or topics.
- Do one chunk or topic at a time.
- If interrupted (especially common at university or within a family) be assertive and keep ad-hoc chats short. Do not be afraid to say you need to get on.

- Put a sign on your door saying 'do not disturb' if necessary.

Many of the techniques and tips in this chapter can also be applied to the work-place. Indeed, time management courses are very common within industry and can help people to cope with and manage deadlines more effectively.

13

Stress in relationships

Personal relationships at home frequently suffer when people work longer hours and have increased demands in what is expected of them. Couples can find they have more fights than laughs, and feel more anger than passion. Often they are simply too exhausted to experience passion. If a person is stressed out in one area of their life, it will usually have an impact on other areas. In this instance the relaxing, comforting place to return after a hard day at work, becomes another chore. Eventually, this can also seriously impact on personal relationships, including the sex-life of the couple concerned. In other words, if stress is not dealt with, a consequence can be the break-up of an important relationship.

The causes of stress in a relationship can be triggered by a number of situations or problems: financial difficulties, illness, incompatibility, work stress, lack of communication, or the presence of children. As has been discussed in earlier chapters, the ways a person can respond under stress are numerous. If you believe you are finding your relationship stressful, or think your partner is feeling stressed about it, it is important you analyse the responses. Are you behaving differently or feeling more angry towards your partner? Are you experiencing the sensations often associated with stress or are you unable to put an image of the two of you separating, out of your head? Are you finding it difficult to concentrate or finding yourself being more short-tempered with your partner? Or are you drinking more alcohol? You may exhibit any number of the stress responses. But once you have identified the main ones, you can begin to focus on and use the techniques and strategies to deal with them. However, below are some general tips on how to deal with stress in a relationship.

Tips on managing relationship stress

- Use your social network for support – are there friends, social groups, colleagues or a GP you can talk to?

- Talk with each other and explore what thoughts are behind the issues.
- Make a list of what you are both stressed or arguing about. Is it the fact that one of you does all the chores? Write a plan to deal with it, for example share the jobs around the house, or swap each week.
- If money is identified as an issue, work on a plan to reduce your out-goings. Perhaps reduce the number of take-aways or analyse whether you need the car?
- Look for joint solutions for a way forward.
- Put time by for each other. If you both work long hours it is too easy to come in, sit down in front of the television, and eat a meal on your lap. Or you find your weekends are taken up with visiting other people or catching up with domestic tasks. It is important you ensure you have quality time together. Commit to a couple of nights per week, and one weekend in three that you keep free for each other.
- If you have children, see whether a family member or friend could look after them for the occasional weekend.
- Talk about what is important to each other. Listen to what each other has to say and do not jump to conclusions or convey your own judgements.
- Share and discuss goals and ambitions. This can help you both focus on a joint future.
- Enjoy socialising – it is important you make time to have fun with other people too!
- Share exercise, jog together, or join a gym. Even if it is only spending a couple hours gardening together or playing a game of tennis in the park.
- Show each other affection. Research has shown that males who kiss their partners every day on leaving home decrease their chances of a heart attack.
- Praise each other and make sure you cuddle one another.

Stress in retirement

Retirement is another period in our journey through life that can put stress on relationships. A couple can often find themselves together all the time for the first time. Before this, the longest they had spent with each other was the two week holiday they took every summer. Now, they do not have a job to disappear to five days a week. And adapting to this change can be stressful. It is no wonder that many people die within a few years of retirement especially if they have experienced a stressful job and do not take early retirement.

Retirement can be additionally stressful if forced due to illness or redundancy. Health problems bring a number of difficulties, as well as feelings of anxiety and worry. Similarly, redundancy can lead to beliefs of failure, or financial concerns. Sitting down and planning the money implications can help to reduce stress if you both have a clear understanding of where you stand financially.

In any of these circumstances, it is important to identify what you like to do together as well as exploring your own hobbies. For example, you could both join an adult education class – you might have different interests but you could enrol at classes on the same day at the same venue. Retirement can be a stage of life to try all those things you have never made the time to do before. If you are able to do so financially and physically, think about going on those holidays you fancied in the past but were never able to take. It is also a time to use your social support network, particularly those in the same situation.

Most importantly, retirement can be a time of huge enjoyment. Any major life change can be perceived as stressful, but by understanding the possible stress responses and techniques to deal with them, retirement can be the beginning of an exciting new phase of your relationship.

14

Stress at work

Stress at work is on the increase. This is in part due to the post-industrial era we live in, characterised by globalisation, corporate reorganisations, the introduction of new technologies and management theories, and an increase in expectations both of the company and its employees.

According to a recent study carried out by Northwestern National Life, an American insurance company, 40% of employees reported their work to be very or extremely stressful (Stress at Work, NIOSH, 1999). This situation is similar in Europe – research published by the European Commission found that over 50% of the 147 million workers who took part in the survey claim to work to a very high speed and to tight deadlines (ESA, Guidance on work-related stress, European Commission, 1999).

These findings support research undertaken at the Centre for Stress Management (Palmer, 2000) that found of the 27% of people who were often or always stressed, work came out on top as the most common stress factor. Taking these statistics into account it is not surprising that about 10 per cent of workers in the United Kingdom, United States, Germany and Finland have depression, anxiety and stress. And in the UK, 30 per cent of employees experience mental health problems at some point in their working life (International Labour Organisation, 2000).

But how is work stress defined? The Health & Safety Executive (2001) defined stress as 'the adverse reaction people have to excessive pressures or other types of demand placed on them'. This is supported by the NIOSH (1999), definition that describes job stress as 'the harmful physical and emotional responses that occur when the requirements of the job do not match the capabilities, resources, or needs of the worker'. As is the case with our earlier definitions of stress (Chapter 1), for example, 'stress occurs when the perceived pressure exceeds your perceived ability to cope', it is important not to confuse job stress with a work challenge. The latter can energise an employee both psychologically and physically, motivate them to learn a new skill or do their job effectively. Stress on the other hand can have a detrimental affect on the way an employee performs at work as well as all the individual responses that can be experienced and the impact these can have on personal lives.

Work-related stress can have major consequences for employers. It can lead to:

- A reduction in employee performance
- A reduction in employee morale
- An increase in absenteeism
- An increase in long-term sick absence. (This can have a spiral effect because once one person is off sick their workload is shared between other employees, which places them under more pressure, thus increasing the chances they may also feel unable to cope)
- An increase in employee turnover or seeking of alternative employment. (Employers are then faced with further recruitment and training costs of new people)
- An increase in industrial relations difficulties
- Increased litigation
- An increase in poor quality control
- A reduction in efficiency
- An increase in accidents
- The existence of the 'long-hours' culture
- An increase in the incidence of bullying
- Employee burnout or 'rust-out'
- An increase in the number of deadlines not being reached

According to the Trade Unions Congress, work-related stress has increased to 6,428 new cases being reported. Hence, in recent years, litigation in the UK has greatly increased for stress-related cases.

What is 'burnout' or 'rust-out'? In simple terms, 'burnout' describes a condition where someone is no longer able to do their job properly because they have experienced too much pressure for too long. They feel physically, emotionally and mentally exhausted. This is common in employees who feel responsible for the well-being and health of other employees. Conversely, rust-out, refers to the situation when an employee experiences too little pressure, or becomes bored due to a fast, repetitive but monotonous job. Both are equally damaging to the health of the individuals. A study carried out by Employment & Social Affairs

(1999) found that 45% of employees that took part in their research had monotonous tasks, 44% had no task rotation, and 50% did short, repetitive tasks.

Some occupations appear to be more stressful than others (Cooper, Dewe and O'Driscoll, 2001). For example, teaching and nursing have some of the highest levels of stress (HSE, 2000).

Companies are now taking work-stress much more seriously and are taking action to deal with it within their organisations. The three key reasons for this are:

1. Employees now have a better understanding of the impact stress can have on their health thus employers are now keener to limit the risks.
2. The law requires employers to tackle work-related stress. There are specific references made in The Health and Safety Laws (Health and Safety at Work Act, 1974 and the Management of Health and Safety at Work Regulations, 1999) that relate to employers taking steps to make sure employees do not suffer stress-related illnesses because of their work. Similarly, there are elements of other laws that may apply to stress such as The Working Time Regulations (1998), The Employment Rights Act (1996) or The Disability Discrimination Act (1995). Recently, there has been a spate of cases where employees have sued employees for causing stress-related illnesses such as clinical depression or anxiety. In 2001 a 27-year-old junior doctor collapsed and died after working an 86-hour week. His parents did not rule out suing the health trust that employed their son. Professor Cary Cooper believes it cannot be long before 'stress-induced death' is actually taken to court as the reason for death. This issue is taken very seriously in Japan.
3. It makes sense economically for an organisation to keep work-stress to a minimum. Whilst it is hard to calculate the true cost of stress on industry, the HSE have estimated that 6.5 million working days were lost in Britain during 1995, due to 'stress, depression, anxiety or a physical condition ascribed to work-related stress – with an average of 16 days off work for each person suffering from the condition' (HSE, 2001). This equates to an overall employee cost of approximately £370 million and £3.75 billion to society as a whole (HSE, 2001, based on 1995/96 prices). However, the Confederation of British Industry estimates the total cost to be about £5.2 billion.

Model of work stress

This section illustrates a model of work stress. This model (Figure 3) has been developed by Palmer and Cooper (Palmer et al., 2001) to include the main hazards covered in the recent Health & Safety Executive recommendations for stress prevention (HSE, 2001).

The model identifies the potential hazards or causes of work stress for employees. Stress is manifested in individual characteristics and organisational symptoms, which lead to negative outcomes for both the individual and the company. This is turn leads to a financial cost for both. In the next section we will focus on the seven hazards and consider how organisations can intervene to reduce or prevent stress.

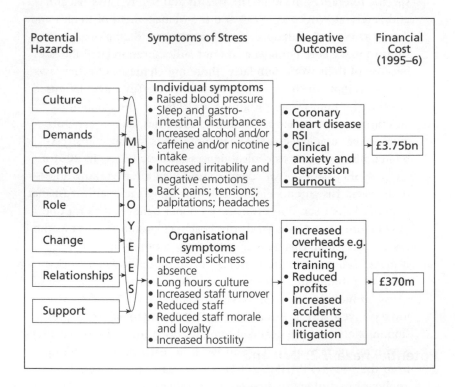

Figure 3: Model of work stress

© Palmer and Cooper, 2001

Potential hazard 1: Culture

The culture of an organisation is crucial in determining how successful it will be in managing work-related stress. Unfortunately, the culture of an organisation is often rigid, rooted in its past, and difficult to change. Companies with a positive culture, that is a company where communication, support, and mutual respect are the norm, are less likely to experience work-related stress.

Use the checklist below to see if you recognise any of these characteristics in your work. These are symptomatic of an unhealthy culture, and one that is likely to experience high levels of stress.

Checklist
* Lack of, or inadequate, open and honest communication
* No stress or well-being policy
* Little opportunity to voice concerns and issues
* Stress or health issues are not treated seriously or dealt with positively
* Lack of consultation or participation in decision-making
* Lack of emotional or practical support
* Little knowledge of company goals, therefore little 'buy in' from employees in the achievements of the organisation
* Problems not recognised or dealt with promptly
* Expectation to work long hours and take work home
* Excessive hierarchy
* Too little or too much supervision
* Existence of racism, sexism, ageism or homophobia
* Inadequate co-ordination
* Inconsistent style of management
* Staff treated with lack of respect or fairness
* Inflexible working procedures

Potential hazard 2: Demands

Demands placed on an individual by his or her employer are often quoted as the main cause of stress. Look at the list below and see if you recognise any of these causes of work stress.

Work overload

This can be defined when a person is allocated a great deal of work, but has insufficient resources (such as staff, time, ability or equipment) to cope with it. Quantitative overload is simply having too much work to complete in the time available. Qualitative overload is work that is too difficult for the employee to undertake because they do not have the capacity, have not had the training, or have an impossible task. Frequently work overload results in employees working excessive hours, which can lead to health problems or relationship problems outside of work (for example, if the employee regularly takes work home). Consistently working excessive hours can cause the employee to become fatigued, which can impact on performance, which in turn can lead to inefficient working practices, resulting in less actually being achieved. This becomes a vicious circle as it perpetuates the stress levels for the individual.

This is different from the occasions when a business has an important deadline to meet and therefore has to work at an extreme level to meet the deadline. If this situation occurs, employees need to understand why it is essential to meet the deadline, know that their extra efforts are appreciated, and know this is not a frequent event. It is also important to recognise the people for the exceptional effort.

Checklist
- Too much work to complete
- Complaints of lack of time or time pressure
- Unrealistic deadlines
- Unable to start or complete task
- Received little or no training to undertake the specific tasks
- Task or job psychologically demanding
- Employee(s) working long hours to complete tasks or projects
- Employee(s) taking work home
- Excessive responsibility
- Insufficient staff to undertake work

Capability and capacity

When entrusting employees with specific tasks it is important to take into account whether or not they are capable of doing it, and that the demands of the job do not exceed their ability to carry out the work in a safe and healthy way. This is a requirement of the Management of Health and Safety at Work Regulations (1999) and includes ensuring the employees' mental health is not put at risk.

Checklist
- Unable to complete task
- Appears confused regarding tasks
- Constantly seeks supervision

Work underload
This is the problem when an employee is not being sufficiently challenged by their job. It is often associated with repetitive, routine, understimulating or boring work and can lead to an employee feeling under-utilised, dissatisfied, and that they are not adding value or making a contribution.

Checklist
- Boring tasks or job
- Routine, repetitive tasks
- Under-stimulated
- Lack of satisfaction
- Low self-worth
- Apathy, low morale
- Lack of responsibility

Physical environment
The environment in which people work can influence the stress levels of employees. Below is a list of some environmental factors intrinsic to stress.

Checklist
- Poor ventilation
- Open-plan offices
- Isolation
- Excessive noise
- Unpredictable loud noises
- Inadequate lighting
- Workplace temperature too hot or too cold
- New technology
- Poorly designed equipment
- Drafty workplace
- Static electricity
- Smoke
- Toxic substances

- Pollution
- VDU screen glare

Exposure to many of these physical demands is quite common. A recent European Commission study found that '25 million European workers are exposed to noise, 8 per cent handle or touch harmful products or substances, 17 per cent report breathing in vapours, fumes or dust during at least half of their working life, 17 per cent report being exposed to vibration, 12 per cent to high and 13 per cent to low temperatures' (Employment & Social Affairs, 1999). Exposure to noise for example, has been associated with headaches, fatigue, reduction in concentration levels and irritability. Whereas vibration, has been found to affect negatively the chemistry and function of the brain (Johanning, Wilder and Landrigan, 1991).

Psychosocial environment
People who deal with the public often experience aggressive, abusive or violent behaviour. This can involve being threatened, sworn at or even physically attacked. Consequently, high staff turnover occurs in places such as call centres.

Checklist
- Violence/abuse
- Lack of personal security
- Poor childcare facilities
- Conflict
- Intimidation
- Abrasive personalities

Potential hazard 3: Control

This hazard relates directly to the amount of control the employee has in how to carry out the work. A recent study (Stansfeld et al., 1999) found that people who had little say in how their work was done had a higher risk of alcohol dependency and an increase in the association of poor mental health. The research also found that people who had an opportunity to participate in decision-making experienced greater job satisfaction and reported higher levels of self-esteem.

Checklist
- Lack of control
- Lack of influence over work
- Lack of autonomy
- Too much supervision
- Lack of involvement in decisions that affect employees

Potential hazard 4: Relationships

Bullying and harassment are two aspects of potential interaction at work that can lead to work-related stress in the same way they can be a cause of stress in children (see Chapter 11). Harassment can be associated with unwanted conduct based on race, religion, gender, origin, disability or nationality. Bullying can be defined as persistent unacceptable behaviour carried out by one or more people against one or more other employees. Bullying can include violence, threatening behaviour, swearing or verbal abuse, the setting of arbitrary or impossible objectives, repeated ridicule or humiliation, withholding information or maliciously preventing career development (Randall, 1997).

Checklist
- Bullying
- Harassment
- Deterioration in, or difficultly in managing, the relationship with manager, team members, colleagues, or customers
- Passive or aggressive managers or colleagues
- Conflicts
- Abrasive personalities
- Office politics
- Lack of social support
- Racism
- Ageism
- Sexism
- Homophobia
- Disability discrimination

Potential hazard 5: Change

There are very few companies which have not undergone significant change in the last decade. Organisational change has increased due to changing market conditions, an increase in competition and products reaching the market faster, the rapid development of new technology, the impact of companies merging, or having to find more cost-effective ways to run. The response has often included downsizing, restructuring and adopting new ways of working. Changes like these can be unsettling and worrying for employees and they can often feel increasingly under pressure. Poor management of change can lead to individuals becoming anxious about their future with the company, and reporting work-related stress.

One of the most important ways to ensure change happens success-fully within your organisation is to ensure that organisations communicate effectively with their employees. Change and transition usually need clear, unambiguous communication with employees, stakeholders, shareholders and customers. If this communication does not occur employees may not understand the objectives of the company and there-fore not understand why the change needs to take place. In these instances staff often experience a reduction in the trust they feel for senior management. The combination of these factors can result in an increase in absenteeism, sickness and staff turnover due to the ambigu-ity experienced by employees. This can cause a reduction in company performance and efficiency.

MORI's figures show that the norm for employees understanding the organization's objectives is 48 per cent, but in periods of change this figure drops to 34 per cent. Similarly, credibility in management drops from 66 per cent to 49 per cent in periods of change.

However, business today has redefined what is expected and required of employees, as companies face a torrent of changes. Organisations have now discovered that in order to achieve their goals and aims they require all employees' energies to be pointing in the same direction. To achieve this, simple compliance from staff is not enough – companies require engagement, loyalty and commitment from their people. All too often, the failure for organisations to change successfully is partly due to a 'disconnect between the communication that the busi-ness needs and the communication it receives' (Quirke, 2001).

In other words, it is imperative during times of change to communicate with employees. Below is a simple checklist of situations for companies to avoid during times of change – notice many of these could be avoided with effective communications with employees.

Checklist
- Employees aware of rumours about impending change
- Little or no communication with staff about change
- Ambiguous communications about possible changes
- Dates and plans for changes not provided
- Staff not involved in changes
- Fears of redundancy
- Senior managers leaving

Potential hazard 6: Role

The role which you have in an organisation can impact on stress levels. It is important for a person's role in an organisation to be clearly defined and understood, and for there not to be any conflict between the expectations placed on them.

Role conflict occurs when an individual has conflicting demands of the job, or is being asked to do tasks that they believe are not part of their role. Employees in this situation often feel torn between two line managers or groups of people, both demanding different types of behaviour or tasks.

Role ambiguity arises when a person is not certain of the expectations of their job and its objectives. This is often the result of a manager not making the job requirements clear, or changes in requirement not being explained. Role ambiguity is most common when an employee changes job, joins a new organisation, is promoted, or has a change in manager.

Checklist
- Employees unsure of their role
- Employees unsure of each others' roles
- Unclear job requirements
- Vague job descriptions
- Unclear objectives
- Employee has more than one line supervisor or manager

Potental hazard 7: Support, training and unique factors

A lack of support and relevant training in the workplace can contribute to stress levels. It is legally necessary for employers to provide sufficient health and safety training for employees but the HSE also recommends that employees receive sufficient training to undertake the core functions of their jobs. It is important for staff to feel comfortable and competent in their roles – this can be achieved by providing training. Similarly, when organisations recruit new members of staff they need to ensure they are as suited to the job as possible in terms of skills, ability and previous experience. Once they commence employment they should receive induction training to make them aware of work policies and also any work-related stress policy, if it exists.

How senior staff support employees is an important factor to managing work-related stress. This can range from how help is provided to employees experiencing difficult events in their lives such as a close bereavement, through to thanking a person for a job well done. If a person is not completing the job to a satisfactory standard it is also important to provide constructive and supportive feedback – pointing out what went wrong and how the person can improve to ensure they complete the task satisfactorily next time.

Catering for unique factors and individual differences is important. Thus young, inexperienced employees may need additional help and assistance adjusting to a new job. Parents with their first baby may experience sleep disturbances and may have a number of personal adjustments to make in their life.

Finally, it is important to bear in mind the dynamics of work teams. Some people thrive on working to tight deadlines, some may enjoy facing customers, yet others prefer to plan in detail their work commitments so they know exactly what needs to be done when. Managers need to take time to understand the people in their teams, ensure they know how their employees like to work, identify their strengths and weaknesses and talk to them as a team. It may be best to allocate tasks dependent on what suits the members of the team, or attempt to manage the work according to the different team members.

Checklist
- Little or no core role training offered
- No staff counselling service or Employee Assistance Programme

- Unsupportive peers
- Unsupportive line management
- Little or no consideration made for individual differences
- Line management make no effort to get to know their staff
- Inadequate feedback

These seven potential hazards: Culture; Demands; Control; Relationships; Change; Role; Support, training and unique factors can all contribute to work-related stress. However, as with the interventions explained in Chapters 3 to 9, there are solutions that can be employed to address the stress-inducing factors. The next section deals with ideas and techniques to reduce stress levels.

Interventions to deal with culture

One of the most important aspects of an organisational culture is regular and effective communications. This is particularly important with the increase in people working from home. Management should communicate in an open and honest way, explaining what is happening and how this will affect their employees. Research has shown that effective communications can help to increase the motivation of employees, decrease staff turnover and consequently improve the performance of the company. A recent survey in 50 countries conducted by Hay Group, a human resources consulting firm, found that over the next two years one-third of the global work force will change employers (Sherman, 2001).

There is no doubt that one of the reasons people will leave a company is because they feel they are not valued and because the company has poor communications practices, in both the interpersonal communications from managers and formal programmes. When the culture is one where people have the information they need in order to perform their jobs, and communication levels are at their optimum across the organisation, 'it stands to reason that employee morale, productivity, effectiveness and efficiency will also be at optimal levels' (Thornton, 2001). In companies with cultures like this, stress levels amongst employees are likely to be reduced. People understand what the company is trying to achieve, why it is trying to achieve it and how they can contribute and consequently they feel supported and valued.

It is also useful to create an environment of involvement by encouraging employees to work with managers and discuss how to tackle work-related stress or emerging problems. Quite often people do not feel able to talk openly about their issues and problems in the workplace because it carries a stigma – therefore by enabling a team to do so encourages a healthier atmosphere. In addition, people feel more relaxed and committed to their job when they understand how they fit into the bigger picture. Involving staff in the planning process helps them to understand the value they are adding.

Finally it is important to provide internal support. This can range from coaching on the job, to welfare services such as counselling for people who experience a personal crisis such as divorce. The degree to which you embrace these issues can play a strong role in developing a culture of committed employees.

Interventions to deal with demands

In order to avoid, or minimise, work overload, it is important to ensure that sufficient resources exist to complete the required work. If there are insufficient resources, line management may need to help staff to prioritise, renegotiate deadlines or recruit more people so the work can be shared accordingly. Conversely, if people perceive they are suffering from work underload, the line manager could consider increasing their responsibility providing they have been given sufficient training. The key is to create a balance between people being busy and motivated but not so overloaded they feel unable to focus on the job. Training can help to create this balance, as can encouraging staff to talk, if they believe that they cannot cope.

In addition companies could share their future plans, the challenges that lie ahead, and what needs to done to meet these. By talking regularly to the staff about these issues, they will start to understand the company's direction and are consequently more committed to helping it to succeed, as they understand the part they play in the equation. On the whole, encourage an environment where long hours and unplanned tight deadlines are not the norm. Finally, it is important to lead by example. There is no point in encouraging a healthy work-life balance, if managers continue to call meetings after the normal hours of work, or send emails to people at weekends or late at night. In other words, it is important that supervisors and managers practise what they preach.

Interventions to deal with control

The best way to provide staff with more control is to enable them to make decisions, plan their own work, and ensure they can use a variety of skills to complete tasks. Another useful method is to hold regular meetings with employees at which the manager can discuss how projects are going and provide advice and support if necessary. This is more effective than constantly monitoring what staff are doing. A supportive environment is essential because employees know they will receive support if things go wrong, and this serves significantly to reduce work-related stress.

Interventions to deal with relationships

Disciplinary and grievance processes and policies can help to provide a framework to deal with unacceptable behaviour such as bullying and harassment. Employees will feel encouraged to know that if an issue like this occurs it will be dealt with and addressed. The procedures and policies can also be drawn up in conjunction with staff and the unions. Once you have established the policies it is important to communicate these and make it clear senior management supports them, as well as explain the consequences of breaching a procedure. However, it is essential to be seen to apply these policies in a consistent manner otherwise staff may believe that they are being unfairly treated.

It is essential to create a feeling of trust, both by the manager demonstrating that he or she trusts the team, and by encouraging them to trust each other. Other team members or management can achieve this through either informal or formal recognition of individual contributions.

Interventions to deal with change

The most important aspect of any change is to explain to people why the change needs to occur. All too often people are not told anything, or told the change is happening and how it might be taking place, but the reasons behind the change are not explained. This results in people not understanding the full picture, meaning they are less committed to supporting the change. This can result in people feeling increased anxiety and apprehension, and being stressed about the outcomes of the change. Management should explain the timescales of the change, why it needs to happen and what the first steps will be, and talk about the impacts on the day-to-day activity. Employees who understand the big picture are more likely to take part in helping the company to succeed. Research (Quirke, 2000) found 84% of employees who understand what makes their business successful want to help to create that success, whereas only 46% of those without that understanding share that belief.

During a time of organisational change, employees are prone to discuss the issues amongst themselves. It is therefore essential to communicate new developments quickly and effectively to avoid the rumour mill spreading inaccurate information. On the whole, people are most interested in how the change is going to impact on them. Will they need to relocate? Will their terms and conditions change? Will their job change? Or will they still have a job? The most effective way to address these questions is through face to face communications. Organisations can provide managers with briefing materials and encourage them to talk to their people in team meetings – this also provides the opportunity for people to ask questions and say what they believe and feel. Encouraging an open-door policy can also encourage people to express their concerns and anxieties and enable senior management to understand the issues better, hence providing more information for improving the way the change is being managed.

Involving staff in the process of change and explaining why the change is taking place will also ensure more people buy into and are committed to the changes. This ensures the overall objectives of the change are more likely to be understood and met. This can be achieved by holding discussion groups to encourage employees to generate ways of solving the problems themselves.

During a time of organisational change it is essential to support employees. If they are being made redundant or laid off, employers could help to give them the skills to find a new job such as interview preparation and helping to write a CV or résumé. Outside consultants are usually employed to offer career guidance and support. Once the change has taken place, employees' objectives will probably need revising in order to avoid role conflict and role ambiguity.

If the aims and objectives were clearly understood for the change, evaluation of whether the process has been successful or not will be easier at a later stage. In fact, it is recommended that the indicators of success are clearly defined at the beginning of the intervention.

Interventions to deal with role issues

It is important to make sure that employees have a clear role. This can be achieved by developing a job description outlining their roles and responsibilities. This can be used as a focus for regular meetings to assess whether the team are still clear about what they are expected to achieve in their job. Expectations from manager to employee and vice versa can be discussed.

When new employees join an organisation, induction training is important. They also need an outline from their manager of what they are expected to do in their jobs.

Interventions to deal with support issues

Creating a supportive environment is vital in reducing work-related stress. This can be achieved by offering encouragement. It is important to listen to staff if problems arise and offer a course of action to address the issues, as well as allowing them to share their concerns. Providing sufficient core role training helps people to develop the skills they need to do the job better. Factors such as a healthy 'work-life' balance and ensuring people take their annual leave entitlement can all contribute to a supportive environment. Organisations need to ensure that they do not discriminate against people on the grounds of race, gender, age or disability. A counselling service may help employees cope with personal problems.

Work-related stress risk assessment

The excellent HSE guide, *Tackling work-related stress: a managers' guide to improving and maintaining employee health and well-being* (2001) provides a structured approach to stress prevention. It provides a five-step work-related stress risk assessment to aid diagnosis of the problem(s) and provide a framework for intervention. The five steps are illustrated below.

STEP 1: Looking for the hazards

- Factor 1: Culture

- Factor 2: Demands
- Factor 3: Control
- Factor 4: Relationships
- Factor 5: Change
- Factor 6: Role
- Factor 7: Support

Use mixture of qualitative and quantitative data gathering methods:

- *QUANTITATIVE:* Productivity and performance data; absence/sickness data; EAP data; staff turnover; questionnaires; stress audits
- *QUALITATIVE*: Focus groups; performance appraisal; informal discussions with staff; return-to-work interviews; exit interviews

STEP 2: Decide who might be harmed and how

- Any employee may suffer from stress regardless of age, status, gender, ethnicity, or disability
- Consider that some staff may be at higher risk at different times

STEP 3: Evaluate the risk and decide if enough is being done

- Consider how factors 1 to 7 in Step 1 could harm the department/unit/division
- Ask: What action is already being taken? Is it enough? If not, what more will you do?
- Attempt to eliminate risks
- Combat risks at organisational level before considering training (stress or pressure management) or counselling.

STEP 4: Record your findings

- If the organisation employs five or more employees, the main findings MUST be recorded
- Findings should be shared with employees

- Use the document to monitor progress especially on particular hazards

STEP 5: Review your assessment and revise where necessary

- Review your assessment whenever significant changes occur in the organisation, or in the way your unit handles its business
- Review in consultation with employees
- Consider reviewing the assessment regularly

We have provided a summary of the five step work-related stress risk assessment approach. Although the approach is not set in stone, it can provide a useful framework for employers wishing to assess and prevent stress in the workplace. Stress prevention at work is usually an on-going process therefore various parts or sections of a large organisation may be at different stages of the five step model. Organisations may need the help of external consultants to undertake different stages, for example, a Registered Safety Practitioner or Chartered Psychologist (see Appendix) may be required to assess stress and undertake a stress or hazard audit. The audit may require specific tools or questionnaires which can be developed for the organisation or commercial stress audit tools may be used instead. We recommend that organisations wishing to prevent or manage work-related stress consider purchasing the recent HSE (2001) documents on stress.

Dealing with work-related stress as an individual

Revisit the first part of this chapter. Tick the items on the hazard checklists that you recognise in your own organisation. Consider the following:

- Is there any action you can take to improve the situation without involving another member of staff?
- Is there any action you can take to improve the situation involving a colleague or line manager?
- Does your organisation have a stress or well being policy? If not, could one be developed?
- Do you have an active Trade Union? If so, are they interested in reducing stress at work?

- Would additional training in core function roles help you or your colleagues?
- Would specific training in stress management or managing pressure be helpful?

Working within one's own organisation to address stress can be difficult depending upon your role or position. If you are not in a managerial, training, occupational health or human resources role, you may need to start by discussing stress prevention with your line manager or peers.

If you now look at yourself, it is useful to assess how you deal with stress or problems that occur at work. For a self-assessment, complete the questionnaire below.

Ideally, a score of 42 or higher is preferable. Look at the items to

Exercise

Coping with work stress questionnaire

When you have a work-related problem or stress to what extent do you do the following?

Helpful behaviour	Never	Rarely	Periodically	Regularly	Very often
Seek support and advice from supervisors	1	2	3	4	5
Try to deal with the situation objectively in an unemotional way	1	2	3	4	5
Try to recognise your own limitations	1	2	3	4	5
Talk to understanding colleagues	1	2	3	4	5
Set priorities and deal with problems accordingly	1	2	3	4	5
Accept the situation and learn to live with it	1	2	3	4	5
Seek as much social support as possible	1	2	3	4	5
Unhelpful behaviour					
'Staying busy'	5	4	3	2	1
'Bottling things up'	5	4	3	2	1
Using distractions (to take your mind off things)	5	4	3	2	1
Smoking more	5	4	3	2	1
Delegate the problem	5	4	3	2	1
Drink alcohol rather more than usual	5	4	3	2	1
Try to avoid the situation	5	4	3	2	1

Plot total score below:

Unhelpful		Helpful
14	42	70

(Adapted from Cooper et al., 1988)

which you allocated a low score. What can you do to improve these low scores?

Enhancing performance

A useful method to improve work performance is to assess what thoughts are interfering with your performance and use the thinking skills you learnt in Chapter 7, to change your interfering thoughts into enhancing thoughts.

Look at the example below and then use the blank half to identify your own performance interfering thoughts and then develop the performance enhancing thoughts (PETs) to address them.

Enhancing performance

Problem: *Meeting a deadline*

Performance Interfering Thinking (PIT)	Performance Enhancing Thinking (PET)
Why can't it be extended?	The deadline isn't going to be extended so I'd better start
Why are they doing this to me?	This is not personal. I work in a high pressure environment
I've got enough to do already	This is true but I need to find the space for a bit more
The deadline's approaching and I haven't done anything yet	Stop procrastinating and start work no matter how irritating it is
Oh Christ!	Charge!
	Other ideas:
	Post-its – Stick on work surfaces with the word 'Charge' written on them.
	Start organizing my time in order to undertake the work to meet the deadline and stop moaning
© Centre for Stress Management, 2002	

Enhancing performance

Problem:

Performance Interfering Thinking (PIT)	Performance Enhancing Thinking (PET)

© Centre for Stress Management, 2002

Conclusion

By using the strategies and techniques outlined in this chapter, you can learn to identify and manage stress in your workplace, as well as deal with your own levels of work-stress. Tackling work-related stress can be complex as a range of stakeholders such as managers, trade unions, employees, health and safety practitioners and external consultants may need to be involved. This provides an interesting challenge and the process is not for the faint hearted. Peer and line manager support will probably be necessary.

15

Using the stress self-assessment questionnaires: a stress self-audit

Now you have almost finished reading this book, you may wish to learn more about yourself and how to reduce your stress levels. This book contained a number of questionnaires to help you assess different aspects of stress. Go back through the book and note down below the scores you obtained for the following questionnaires:

Questionnaire	Score
Personality and behavioural variables	
• Type A, Type B (pages 18–19)	_____
• Locus of Control (page 15)	_____
• Life Event Score (pages 9–10)	_____
Stress Moderators	
• Social support, personal problems (page 74)	_____
• Social support, work problems (page 75)	_____
• Coping with life stress (pages 25–26)	_____
• Coping with work stress (pages 128–129)	_____

Now compare your profile with Figure 4 on page 133. We have provided examples ranging from low to high vulnerability to stress. Does your profile look similar to one of those illustrated in Figure 4?

It is important to note that you are in a position to change your scores by taking decisive action in different areas relating to stress. For example, if you have a high Type A score, it is important to consider how to modify the behaviour. If you have a low social support score, you may wish to increase your support network and if you have a low coping with work stress score you may wish to recognise your limitations and set priorities.

Revisit different sections in the book that focus on areas that you may wish to deal with or change. It is worth rescoring the questionnaires every three months to notice how you are progressing. Although you may be attempting to improve your profile, do not be surprised that occasionally you lapse. This will often occur during times of stress. However, skills practice within the seven BASIC I.D. modalities will help you to improve your stress management abilities.

Plot your scores below and join up a line between them:

Personality and behavioural variables

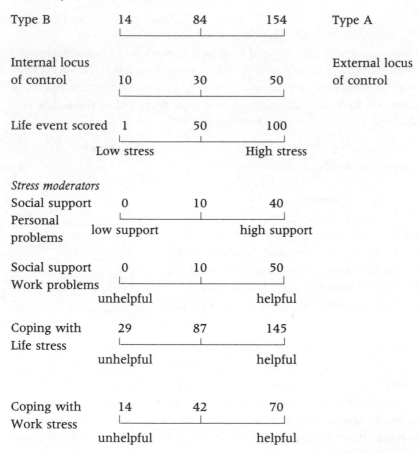

| Type B | 14 | 84 | 154 | Type A |

| Internal locus of control | 10 | 30 | 50 | External locus of control |

| Life event scored | 1 | 50 | 100 |
Low stress   High stress

Stress moderators

| Social support Personal problems | 0 | 10 | 40 |
low support   high support

| Social support Work problems | 0 | 10 | 50 |
unhelpful   helpful

| Coping with Life stress | 29 | 87 | 145 |
unhelpful   helpful

| Coping with Work stress | 14 | 42 | 70 |
unhelpful   helpful

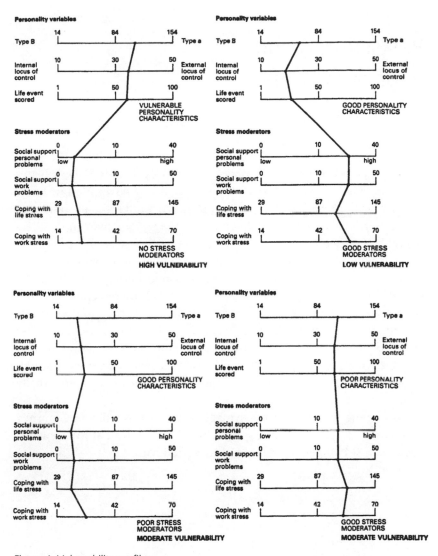

Figure 4: Vulnerability profiles

© Cooper et al., 1988

Postscript: Being your own stress management coach

Having read all or part of this book we hope you now have a better understanding of what stress is, the impact it can have on your body, and a range of techniques to deal with it. We would like to think that the strategies outlined will help you to manage your lives more effectively, both at work and home.

It is important to remember that we are likely to experience stressful events throughout our lives. But we hope by applying the skills included in this book you will be able to deal with them better. And also we acknowledge that you will all face challenges throughout your life, indeed, we would argue these are healthy. Without them you may never apply for that new job, start or finish a relationship, or revise for that exam. If you perceive yourself in control, you will be able to deal with these situations in different ways and coach yourself so you actually enjoy your life more.

Becoming your own stress management coach is a life long journey of discovery as you challenge your own behaviours and attitudes which have been stress-creating instead of stress-reducing.

Bon Voyage!

Appendix

American Counselling Association
5999 Stevenson Avenue
Alexandria
VA 22304-3300
USA

Administration: +(1) 703 823 8900
Website: www.counseling.org
Provides information on counsellors in the USA.

American Psychological Association
1200 17th Street, NW
Washington
DC 20036
USA

Administration: +(1) 202 955 7600
Website: www.apa.org
US equivalent of British Psychological Society.

Australian Psychological Society
PO Box 38
Flinders Lane Post Office
Melbourne
Victoria 8009
Australia

Administration: +61 (3) 8662 3300
Email: contactus@psychsociety.com.au
Website: aps.psychsociety.com.au
Provides information on psychology and
counselling in Australia.

**British Association for Behavioural and
Cognitive Psychotherapies**
PO Box 9
Accrington
BB5 2GD
England

Administration: +44 (0) 1254 875277
Website: www.babcp.org.uk
Holds a registered of accredited cognitive-
behavioural therapists. This approach is similar
to the approach advocated by this book.

**British Association for Counselling and
Psychotherapy**
1 Regent Place
Warwickshire
CV21 2PJ
England

Administration: +44 (0) 1788 550899
Information: 44 (0) 1788 578328
Website: www.bac.co.uk
Holds a register of accredited counsellors.

British Psychological Society
St Andrews House
48 Princes Road East
Leicester
LE1 7DR
England

Administration: +44 (0) 116 254 9568
Website: www.bps.org.uk
Holds a register of chartered psychologists.

**British Society of Experimental and Clinical
Hypnosis**
Hon. Secretary Ann Williamson
Hollybank House
Lees Road
Mossley
Ashton-under-Lyne
OL5 0PL
England

Aministration: +44 (0) 1457 839 363
Fax: as above
Email honsec@bsech.com
Website: www.bsech.com
Holds register of psychologists who practise
hypnosis.

Centre for Coaching
156 Westcombe Hill
London
SE3 7DH
England

Administration: +44 (0) 20 8318 4448
Website: www.centreforcoaching.com

Provides a coaching and training programme
using the approach advocated by this book.

Centre for Stress Management
PO Box 26583
London
SE3 7EZ
England

Administration: +44 (0) 20 8318 5653
Fax: +44 (0) 20 8297 5656
Website: www.managingstress.com

Provides stress management coaching and
counselling. Provides training for personnel and
health professionals and undertakes stress
audits. It runs distance learning programmes
and stress management courses using the
approach advocated by this book.

Health & Safety Executive
Enquiries
Caerphilly Business Park
CF83 3GG
Wales

Administration: +44 (0) 8701 545 500
Fax: +44 (0) 2920 859 260
Email: hseinformationservices@natbrit.com
Website: www.hse.gov.uk

Provides information on all health and safety
issues.

**Institution of Occupational Safety and
Health**
The Grange
Highfield Drive
Wigston
Leicestershire
LE18 1NN
England

Administration: +44 (0) 116 257 3100
Fax: +44 (0) 116 257 3101
Website: www.iosh.co.uk

Holds a register of safety practitioners.

**International Stress Management
Association (UK)**
PO Box 348
Waltham Cross
EN8 8XL
England

Administration: +44 (0) 7000 780430
Website: www.isma.org.uk

Provides information about stress management,
runs National Stress Awareness Day (UK), and
accredits members.

**National Institute for Occupational Safety
and Health (NIOSH)**
4676 Columbia Parkway
Cincinnati
OH 45226-1988
USA

Administration: +1 800 356 4674
Fax: +1 513 533 8573
Website: www.cdc.gov/niosh

Provides information about US occupational
health and safety.

Robertson Cooper Ltd
The Fairbarn Building
UMIST
PO Box 88
Manchester
M60 QD
England

Administration: +44 (0) 161 200 4562
Consultancy which provides a stress auditing
service.

References

Aurelius, M. (1995). *Meditations* (abridged by R. Waterfield). London: Penguin Books.

Beck, A. T. (1993). Cognitive approaches to stress, in P. M. Lehrer and R. L. Woolfolk (eds), *Principles and Practice of Stress Management*, 2nd edition. New York: Guilford Press.

Benson, H. (1976). *The Relaxation Response*. London: Collins.

Bor, R., Josse, J. and Palmer, S. (2000). *Stress-Free Flying*. Dinton: Mark Allen Publishing.

Bortner, R. W. (1969). A short rating scale as a potential measure of pattern A behaviour, *Journal of Chronic Diseases*, 22: 87–91.

Bowlby J. (1969). *Attachment and loss*. Vol. 1: *Attachment*. New York: Basic Books.

Clarke, D. and Palmer, S. (1994). *Stress Management Trainer's Guide*. Cambridge: National Extension College.

Cooper, C. L., Cooper, R. D., and Eaker, L. H. (1988). *Living with Stress*. London: Penguin Health.

Cooper, C. L., Dewe, P. and O'Driscoll, M. (2001). *Organisational Stress*. California and London: Sage.

Cooper, C. L. and Palmer, S. (2000). *Conquer Your Stress*. London: CIPD.

Earnshaw, J. and Cooper, C. (1996). *Stress and Employer Liability*. London: IPD.

Ellis, A. (1997). The future of cognitive-behavior and rational emotive behavior therapy. In S. Palmer and V. Varma (eds), *The Future of Counselling and Psychotherapy*. London: Sage.

Ellis, A. (2001). *Feeling Better, Getting Better, Staying Better: Profound Self-therapy for your Emotions*. Atascadero, CA: Impact Publishers.

Ellis, A., Gordon, J., Neenan, M. and Palmer, S. (1997). *Counselling: a Rational Emotive Behaviour Approach*. London: Continuum.

Employment and Social Affairs (1999). *Health and Safety at Work. Guidance on Work Related Stress – Spice of Life – or Kiss of Death?* Luxembourg: European Commission.

Friedman, M. and Rosenman, R. H. (1974).*Type A Behavior and Your Heart*. New York: Knopf Wildwood House.

Geddes and Grosset (1999). *Achieving Relaxation*. New Canark, Scotland: Geddes & Grosset.

Gregson, O. and Looker, T. (1996). The biological basis of stress management. In S. Palmer and W. Dryden (eds), *Stress Management and Counselling: Theory, Practice, Research and Methodology*. London: Cassell.

Griffiths, R. R. and Woodson, P. (1988). Caffeine physical dependence: a review of human and laboratory animal studies, *Psychopharmacology*, 94: 437–51.

Health and Safety Executive (2000). *The Scale of Occupational Stress: a Further Analysis of the Impact of Demographic Factors and Job Type*. Suffolk: HSE.

Health and Safety Executive (2001). *Tackling Work Related Stress: a Managers' Guide to Improving and Maintaining Employee Health and Well-being*. Suffolk: HSE.

International Labour Organisation (2000). *Mental Health in the Workplace*. Geneva: International Labour Organisation.

International Stress Management Association (2000). *New technology not to blame as stress figures soar*. http://www.isma.org.uk/pr06.htm

Johanning, E., Wilder, D. G. and Landrigan, P. J. (1991). Whole-body vibration exposure in subway cars and review of adverse health effects, *Journal of Occupational Medicine*, 33 (5), 605–612.

Lazarus, A. A. (1977). Toward an egoless state of being. In A. Ellis and R. Grieger (eds), *Handbook of Rational-Emotive Therapy*. New York: Springer.

Lazarus, A. A. (1984). *In the Mind's Eye*. New York: Guilford Press.

Lazarus, A. A. (1989). *The Practice of Multimodal Therapy*. Altimore, MD: The John Hopkins University Press.

Lazarus, A. A. (1997). *Brief but Comprehensive Psychotherapy: the Multimodal Way*. New York: Springer Publishing Company.

Lazarus, R. S. (1999). *Stress and Emotion: a New Synthesis*. London: Free Association Books.

Lazarus, R.S. and Folkman, S. (1984). *Stress, Appraisal and Coping*. New York: Springer.

Leonard, B.E. and Miller, K. (1995). *Stress, the Immune System and Psychiatry*. Chichester: John Wiley & Sons.

Lindenfield, G. (1986). *Assert Yourself: a Self-Help Assertiveness Programme for Men and Women*. Wellingborough: Thorsons.

Marks, I. M. (1980). *Living with Fear*. New York: McGraw-Hill.

Marks, I. M. (1986). *Behavioural Psychotherapy: Maudsley Pocket Book of Clinical Management*. Bristol: Wright.

McMullin, R. E. (1986). *Handbook of Cognitive Therapy Techniques*. New York: Norton.

National Institute for Occupational Safety and Health (1999). *Stress at Work*. US: NIOSH.

Neenam, M. and Dryden, W. *Life Coaching: a Cognitive-Behavioural Approach*. Hove: Brunner-Routledge.

Palmer, S. (1988). *Personal Stress Management Programme Manual*. London: Centre for Stress Management.

Palmer, S. (1989). The use of stability zones, rituals and routines to reduce or prevent stress, *Stress News*, 1(3): 3–5.

Palmer, S. and Dryden, W. (1991). A multimodal approach to stress management. *Stress News*, 3, (1): 2–10.

Palmer, S. (1993). *Multimodal Techniques: Relaxation and Hypnosis*. London: Centre for Stress Management and Centre for Multimodal Therapy.

Palmer, S. and Dryden, W. (1995). *Counselling for Stress Problems*. London: Sage.

Palmer, S. (1996). The multimodal approach: theory, assessment, techniques and interventions. In S. Palmer and W. Dryden (eds), *Stress Management and Counselling: Theory, Practice, Research and Methodology*. London: Cassell.

Palmer, S. and Strickland, L. (1996). *Stress Management: a Quick Guide*. Dunstable: Folens.

Palmer, S. (1997a). Stress counselling and management: past, present and future. In S. Palmer and V. Varma (eds), *The Future of Counselling and Psychotherapy*. London: Sage.

Palmer, S. (1997b). Self-acceptance: concept, techniques and interventions. *The Rational Emotive Behaviour Therapist*, 5, 1: 48–51.

Palmer, S. and Neenan, M. (1998). Double imagery procedure. *The Rational Emotive Behaviour Therapist*, 6, 2: 89–92.

Palmer, S. (2000). *Stress Management – a Masterclass: Professorial Inaugural Lecture*. London: City University.

Palmer, S. and Dryden, W. (1991). A multimodal approach to stress management, *Stress News*, 3 (1): 2–10.

Palmer, S., Cooper, C. L. and Thomas, K. (2001). Model of organisational stress for use within an occupational health education/promotion or wellbeing programme – a short communication. *Health Education Journal*, 60 (4), 378–380.

Parrot, A. (1991). Social drugs: their effects upon health, in M. Pitts and K. Phillips (eds), *The Psychology of Health: an Introduction*. London: Routledge.

Quirke, B. (2000). *Making the Connections – Using Internal Communication to Turn Strategy into Action*. Aldershot: Gower.

Randall, P. (1997). *Adult Bullying: Perpetrators and Victims. London*: Routledge.

Rosenman, R.H., Brand, R.J., Jenkins, C.D., Friedman, M., Straus, R. and Wurm, M. (1975). Coronary heart disease in the Western Collaborative Group Study: Final follow-up experience of 8.5 years. *Journal of the American Medical Association*, 22, 872–7.

Rotter, J. B. (1966). Generalised expectancies for internal versus external control of reinforcement, *Psychology Monographs: General and Applied*, 80, 1–26.

Ruiz-Bueno, J. (2000). Locus of control, perceived control, and learned helplessness, in V. Hill Rice (ed), *Handbook of Stress, Coping, and Health: Implications for Nursing Research, Theory, and Practice*. Thousand Oaks: Sage.

Sherman, D. (2001). The Retention Dilemma: 'Why Productive Workers Leave – Seven Suggestions for Keeping Them'. London: HayGroup.

Stansfeld, S., Head, J., and Marmot, M. (1999). *Work Related Factors and Ill Health*, The Whitehall II Study. Suffolk: HSE.

Thornton, S.L. (2001). How communication can aid retention. *Strategic Communication Management*, Vol. 5, Issue 6, 24–27.

Toates, F. (1995). *Stress: Conceptual and Biological Aspects*. Chichester: John Wiley & Sons.

White, J. (2000). *Treating Anxiety and Stress: a Group Psychoeducational Approach Using Brief CBT*. Chichester: John Wiley & Sons.

Index